don't talk
about it -
Do It

Grant G. Gard

don't talk about it - Do It

grant g. gard
omaha, nebraska

Published by:

Gard & Company

P.O. Box 34579

Northwest Station

Omaha, Nebraska 68134

First Printing	August	1974
Second Printing	October	1974
Third Printing	December	1976
Fourth Printing	September	1978
Fifth Printing	March	1979 (Revised)
Sixth Printing	September	1981
Seventh Printing	December	1983

ISBN 0-9603316-0-3

In Memory of My Son, Gregory

March 2, 1954 — September 24, 1971

and
In appreciation to my wife,
Anita

Introduction

CONGRATULATIONS for being the type of person who is seeking additional ideas to increase your happiness and effectiveness!

A person cannot accomplish anything greater than that which he is. The very determined person finds a way; the other kind finds an excuse. The purpose of this book is to provide you with some basic ideas to help you find a way for further achievement and happiness. School is never out for the Pro. Learning is a continuing process. Personal development becomes the key to unlock the door to the stairway leading to more happiness and achievement. Everything starts with you and how well you can handle situations and people.

It's your *attitude* even more than your *aptitude* that will determine your *altitude* in life. Nothing can stop the person who is filled with the right type of attitude. Nothing can help the person filled with the wrong type of attitude.

I want you finishing this book with this kind of positive, optimistic attitude. . . . Sam was taking up parachuting. He called his friend Charlie, a pilot, to take him up for his first jump. When they got up to 5,000 feet Charlie said, "Sam, have you got your chute on tight? . . . Got your CB strapped on and turned on so we can communicate in case you get in trouble?" Sam replied that everything was in order. Charlie pushed Sam out. In a few seconds Charlie looked down and Sam was at 2,500 feet and the chute was not opened. Charlie yelled down on the CB, "Sam, pull the cord, you are at 2,500 feet!" Sam replied, "No way, Charlie, too much fun!" Shortly, Sam had fallen to 1,000 feet above the ground and still no chute. Charlie told Sam to open the chute and Sam replied again that it was just too much fun. Charlie looked down again and Sam was at 15 feet above the ground and still he had not opened his chute. Charlie turned white with fear and yelled down on the CB, "Mayday, Mayday, Sam pull the cord quick. You are only 15 feet above the ground." Sam looked up and said, "No way, Charlie, I can jump from here!" That kind of optimism and positive attitude eliminates fear and self-doubt and enables people to accomplish greater things.

Also, we are going to be discussing the biggest problem that you and I face each day and that is getting DESIRED results in dealing with people. We always get some kind of results—but I said "getting *desired* results."

Recently it was reported that a president of a leading baking company in the midwest was asked something like this, "How are things in the baking business?" The president replied, "As far as the pies, the cakes and various doughs are concerned, things are great, BUT people keep getting in the way!"

The biggest thing you have standing in the way of achieving your goals boils down to "people"—they keep getting in our way, so I will try to give you some ideas to help in dealing with this challenge.

We have to be able to turn the minuses into pluses . . . reminds me of the story of the little kid who had a pet turtle. Gee, he loved that turtle! Every morning he would look in the box where the turtle slept and feed the turtle and then off to school he would go. Well, this one morning he started to feed the turtle, looked down in the box and found that the turtle was dead. The little kid began to cry and finally the father said, "Son, you quit crying, go to school, cooperate with the teacher, get your lessons, then at four o'clock when school is over you can invite all of your friends in for a real funeral procession. We'll bury that turtle in grand style and as soon as we have the turtle buried I am going to have all of you kids in for ice cream and cake and as soon as we have the ice cream and cake eaten I am going to take all of you to the movies."

The little kid quit crying and his eyes began to get the size of silver dollars . . . real excited . . . then he happened to glance down in the box and the turtle that he thought was dead was really only sleeping. The little kid looked up at his Dad and said, "Let's kill him, Dad." Yes, it's the mark of a pro to be able to handle the human situations that come up daily and handle them in such a way that we motivate people to do the thing we know should be done.

Minds are like parachutes . . . they only function when they are open. PLEASE have an open mind when you read this book. That is the only way that this book can help you. Remember that soap never got anything clean until it was applied. None of these principles will help until they are applied. So let's DON'T TALK ABOUT IT . . . let's move right to Chapter One.

Contents

don't talk about it - Do It

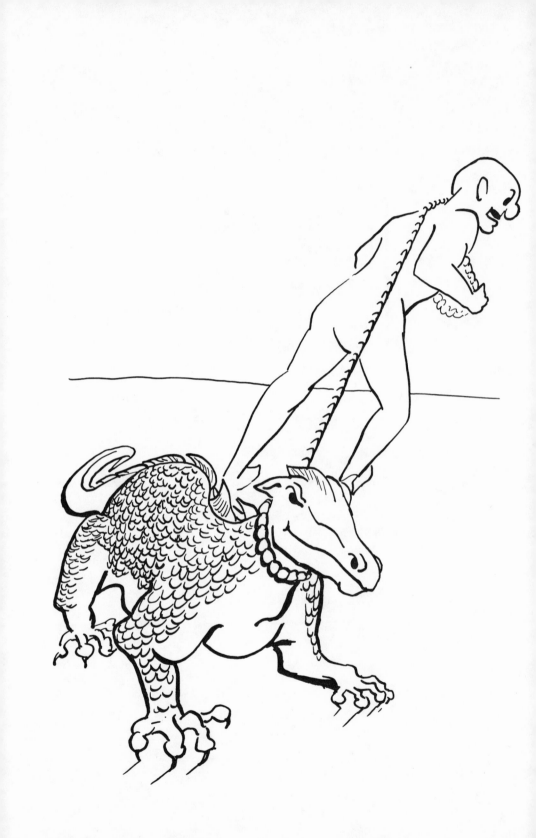

1 | *Courage and Determination— Essential Elements*

You Have Everything You Really Want. Right now, everyone of us has everything we really want. I didn't say "dreamed about" and I didn't say "wished for" . . . but I did say "REALLY WANT." When you want a thing really badly enough, you will find a way. The very DETERMINED person finds a WAY, the other kind finds an EXCUSE. It appears many of the people are standing around waiting for THEIR SHIP TO COME IN . . . THE PROBLEM IS THEY HAVEN'T SENT ONE OUT! You get back exactly what you have sent out . . . bad or good, constructive or destructive.

Many people are hoping for that BIG BREAK that will give them instant fast fame, fortune, happiness and all the things they want from life. They are always dreaming and wishing for someone else's success, achievement, ability, position or talent. When I am speaking at various conventions on any coast line, I enjoy taking a stroll up the seashore and walking on the docks. Silently, I stand there watching the masses of people and wonder how

3

many of them are looking out to the ocean hoping their ship is on the way IN. Yet I know, and deep down inside they know, their ship has NEVER LEFT PORT, they simply haven't sent one OUT. Their ship is still anchored, motionless, going nowhere, just waiting for them to take positive action to bring in positive results.

WHAT'S AROUND YOU IS YOU

You always get back in life exactly what you send out! In my career as a professional speaker and trainer of personal development, I'm in front of all kinds of people daily . . . leaders, housewives, salespeople, farmers, people from all walks of life. Some of the most tragic things I hear are, "If only I had John's leadership ability; if only I could sing like Mary; if only I could sell like Jack; if only the time was right for me to start my self-improvement (there is never a 'just right time for anything'— make the time right); if only I could get a promotion like Jim did." People who feel like that are members of what I call the "IF ONLY" club!!

I firmly believe that every man or woman on the face of this earth can do the things in life that he or she REALLY WANTS TO DO. You have everything RIGHT NOW to do the things with your life that you really want to do and to become the type of person that you really want to become.

USE IT or you'll LOSE IT. This is true about everything in life. I have seen thousands of people who DIDN'T succeed, but I've never seen an individual who COULDN'T succeed if he or she would apply a few simple "RULES AND TECH-NIQUES" and be willing to pay the price to BREAK OUT OF HIS OR HER COMFORT ZONE. Success comes in CANS . . . failure comes in CAN NOTS. GOD has given you all of the abilities and the tools necessary for you to PLACE AROUND YOU all of the POSITIVE, DELIGHTFUL CIRCUMSTANCES that you WANT AROUND YOU. Right now think only in "I CAN" thoughts and discard any "I CAN NOT" thoughts that you may be holding.

HAVE A STRONG PURPOSE

T. T. Munger said, "There is no road to success, but through a clear, strong purpose. Nothing can take its place. A purpose underlies character, culture, position, attainment of every sort."

Become outstanding in your job—become as good as you can at the thing you are doing now. Nothing will take the place of a "strong purpose." Have a strength of character so strong and determined that you are moving in the RIGHT DIRECTION FOR YOU at all times!

To quote Carlyle: "A man with a half-volition goes backwards and forwards and makes no way on the smoothest road; a man with a whole volition advances on the roughest and will reach his purpose, if there be even a little wisdom in it."

Decide your exact purpose, be strong-willed and fire all of your volleys!! You'll achieve the GOALS of your life.

LOOK FOR YOUR SPARK OF INDIVIDUALITY

"All Fords are exactly alike," their maker, Henry Ford, used to say, "but no two men are just alike. Every new life is a new thing under the sun; there has never been anything just like it before, and never will be again. A young man ought to get that idea about himself; he should look for the SINGLE SPARK OF INDIVIDUALITY THAT MAKES HIM DIFFERENT from other folks, and develop that for all he is worth. Society and schools may try to iron it out of him; their tendency is to put us all in the same mold, but I say don't let that spark be lost; IT'S YOUR ONLY CLAIM TO IMPORTANCE."

Sell yourself on yourself and your abilities. Be thankful you are you. Believe that you CAN SUCCEED and have GREAT and GOOD THINGS AROUND YOU. You must believe that your situation and all your future situations are in the grasp of your hands.

THE CHOICE IS YOURS

The story is told about the elderly wise man who was a genius. He was said to be able to answer any question that was ever asked of him. One day, a small boy thought he could fool this wise man, so he caught a small bird in his hands and headed for the wise man's house. The boy was holding the bird in his hands behind his back so the wise man couldn't see. He told the wise man he had a bird in his hands, but he asked the wise old fellow if the bird was dead or alive. Without any pause at all, the wise man said, "Young man, if I say that the bird is alive you will close your hands and crush him to death. If I say the bird is dead you will open your hands and he will fly away. You see, young fellow, IN YOUR HANDS YOUR *WILL* WILL BE DONE." In *your* hands you have everything that you really need . . . it's *your choice* that will determine everything you will do in life!!

THANK GOD FOR YOUR PROBLEMS

The biggest obstacles standing between you and your goals simply boils down to the problems and the adversities that you face. Every successful man or woman has faced many, many problems and setbacks. In fact, problems and adversities are the

VERY FACTORS that make people successful. They become stepping stones to greater achievement when you recognize adversities for what they really are . . . OPPORTUNITIES FOR US TO SUCCEED!

After I spoke to a National Convention in New Orleans, a lady walked up to me and said, "Mr. Gard, you sound as though you never have had a problem in this world! Have you ever had any problems or adversities in your life?" I assured her, and I assure everyone who reads this book, that I have had my share of problems, adversities and setbacks. You see, I have been as low and down in the dumps as a person can possibly be. I have had a bank balance of 73 cents, with a stack of bills to pay out of my next pay check and that next pay check was two weeks off. I have become so depressed that I have mentally resigned my job several times. Yes, and for a short period in my life, I was a Charter Member and President of the "IF ONLY" club. Then one day early in my career I made a real important discovery . . . YOU DON'T DROWN BY FALLING IN THE WATER, YOU ONLY DROWN IF YOU STAY THERE.

These periods in my life were good for me. They were my FAITH BUILDING PERIODS making me a much stronger and bigger person.

It's all right to get down, but NEVER get down on yourself! You are not beaten by being KNOCKED DOWN. You are only beaten if you STAY DOWN. I feel we should thank God for the problems and adversities we have because they are OPPORTUNITIES for our growth!

TURN ADVERSITY INTO ACHIEVEMENT

Have Courage and Determination to Face Adversity. A lad was born in Kentucky over a century ago. He spent most of his youth clerking in a store in Illinois. This young fellow, throughout his life, probably didn't have over a year of formal education. One day he attended an auction where he purchased a barrel of junk for fifty cents. In the whole barrel there wasn't anything of real value except two books—law books.

This young fellow read those books from cover to cover many, many times. Sometimes he would read in the evening by the crackling fire of the fireplace and again early in the morning in his cold bed by the light that shone between the cracks in the log cabin in which he and his family lived. He read and he read, preparing himself, knowing that someday, with preparation and courage, his time would come.

In his younger days he often would walk thirty to forty miles to hear a famous speaker. He would come home so stirred, so determined to be a speaker that he would practice for hours. He would study the careers of famous speakers and practice and more practice.

I have heard it said that he would walk as far as fifty miles to get his hands on a book which he had not read. He was willing to PAY THE PRICE to bring his PLANNED GOALS into a REALITY. His time did come.

His remains will forever rest in a magnificent tomb in Springfield, Illinois . . . a place that is visited by thousands of people each year. He was the sixteenth President of the United States, his name . . . Abraham Lincoln.

Because of his keen insight, his profound depth of character, his DETERMINATION, and his COURAGE to drive on in the FACE OF ADVERSITY, he endeared himself to millions all over the world. Let's take a look at his record and honestly evaluate how we would have reacted if we had faced the many adversities Abraham Lincoln faced and still he came out on top.

Abraham Lincoln's record is as follows:
Lost job 1832.
Defeated for Legislature 1832.
Failed in business 1833.
Elected to Legislature 1834.
Sweetheart died 1835.
Had nervous breakdown 1836.
Defeated for Speaker 1838.
Defeated for nomination for Congress 1843.
Elected to Congress 1846.
Lost renomination 1848.
Rejected for Land Officer 1849.
Defeated for Senate 1854.
Defeated for nomination for Vice-President 1856.
Again defeated for Senate 1858.
Elected President 1860.

We have to prepare ourselves well in advance of the time that opportunity knocks, otherwise we will probably not see the opportunity or be able to capitalize on opportunity.

PREPARE DAILY

A person who doesn't read a book is no better than one who can't read. A person who doesn't listen to tapes is no better than one who doesn't care. School is never out for the Pro. Learning is a continuing process. Many say that experience is the best teacher. I don't believe so—the tuition is too high and costly. Learn from other peoples' experiences. Take advantage of their mistakes and their successes. Read and listen to what others have learned. Attend every lecture, seminar and workshop that you can. Read, listen and absorb all of the "learning" that you possibly can.

One generation takes up where the last one leaves off. One of the basic keys to success is to profit from others' experiences. Oddly enough it's the person who knows everything who has the most to learn.

You should make a list of the things you should do daily, weekly, and monthly to prepare yourself for "*Your Time.*"

Abraham Lincoln prepared himself, knew what he wanted from life, overcame adversities, had the courage to drive on and his time did come.

I firmly believe that God has given us the tools to do the things with our lives that we really want to do. It's up to us to use and develop our abilities.

I know of a young man in Colorado who decided exactly what he wanted to accomplish. In 1963, when I first met this man, he had his office and manufacturing facilities in his garage. His employees consisted of his wife and about 5 or 6 people. The last contact I had with this man in 1970, he was President of his company, had about 200 employees, had just built a new, beautiful plant and had not only taken his product nationwide, but also international. Growing every day!

He is working hard to improve every phase of his operation every day and is constantly coming out with a new "model." He decided what he wanted, went after it like a bulldog going after a cat and he succeeded!

If you aren't satisfied with your present status in life, and I do hope everyone has what I call "HAPPY DISCONTENT-MENT"—that's where you are looking for ways and means to do even better, you can change your life by changing your thoughts.

Emerson wrote: "What a new face courage puts on everything. A determined man, by his very attitude and the tone of his voice, puts a stop to defeat and begins to conquer."

You must FIRST DETERMINE what it is that you really want from life, PREPARE YOURSELF, have DETERMINATION and COURAGE to go after it without PROCRASTINATION, and realize that FAILURE IS NEVER FATAL.

When you're lost in the world, and you're scared as a child,
And death looks you bang in the eye,
And you're sore as a boil, it's according to Hoyle
To cock your revolver and . . . die.
But the code of a man says: "Fight all you can,"
And self-dissolution is barred.
In hunger and woe, oh, it's easy to blow . . .
It's the hell-served-for breakfast that's hard.

You're sick of the game! "Well, now, that's a shame."
You're young and you're brave and you're bright.
"You've had a raw deal!" I know—but don't squeal.
Buck up, do your damnedest, and fight.
It's the plugging away that will win you the day,
So don't be a piker, old pard!
Just draw on your grit; it's so easy to quit;
It's the keeping-your-chin-up that's hard.

It's easy to cry that you're beaten—and die.
It's easy to crawfish and crawl;
But to fight and to fight when hope's out of sight,
Why, that's the best game of them all!
And though you come out of each grueling bout
All broken and beaten and scarred,
Just have one more try—it's dead easy to die,
It's the keeping-on-living that's hard.

—Robert W. Service

Make the poem of Robert Service part of you, read it first

thing in the morning; when the going gets tough—make it part of your "nervous system."

Marshal Foch said, "Ninety thousand conquered men retire before ninety thousand conquering men only because they have had enough, because they no longer believe in victory, because they are demoralized—at the end of their moral resistance."

What he is saying is that the retiring men are not whipped physically, but they are whipped mentally—they no longer have COURAGE, DRIVE, AMBITION and CONFIDENCE. There is no hope for any group of men like that nor is there any hope for a man like that.

Chaplain Frazier, a ranking Chaplain in the first World War, was asked the requirements essential for the success of a Navy Chaplain. His reply was: "Grace, Gumption, Grit and Guts."

Those are the requirements to forge ahead as a salesman, businessman, clergyman, housewife . . . The basics for anyone.

PAY THE PRICE FOR SUCCESS AND HAPPINESS

There was a young musician who played in one of the finest symphony orchestras in Europe. Times were difficult and jobs were hard to come by and a job with an orchestra was a fantastic thing.

This young man was on his way up when suddenly disaster, for a musician, seemed to strike. He began to lose his eyesight. He was afraid that it might be discovered and he would lose his fine job, so secretly he began to take his music home and memorize it note for note. Soon he started in on the music belonging to other members of the orchestra and after a while he not only knew his music by heart, but also that of every member of the orchestra.

He became one of the truly outstanding members of the

orchestra and still no one was completely aware of the condition of his eyes. He had prepared himself for the future—when he wouldn't be able to see.

One night the conductor became ill and the young man was asked to conduct this great orchestra. He approached the podium, grasped the baton, reached over and closed the conductor's score. That night he conducted the symphony without having to look at a single note.

He had been a success because he was willing to pay the price to prepare for this opportunity. He went on to become one of the noted conductors of symphonies throughout the world. His name, Arturo Toscanini.

It is known that there is a price that must be paid for success and happiness. Successful people have been prepared when the opportunity came. We must not quit because of adversities, but we must become stronger and even better people as the result of difficulties and have the COURAGE and DETERMINATION to be prepared for our time—OUR GREAT OPPORTUNITY. IN THE DIFFICULTY LIES THE OPPORTUNITY!

DECIDE NOW WHAT YOU WANT FROM LIFE

An old sage lived in a cabin at the edge of a lake just a short distance from town. One day, he was sitting on his front porch in his rocking chair just gazing down the path and out over the lake. As he gazed, he became aware of a small boy making his way up the path to his cabin. When the boy arrived, he stopped rocking and said, "Lad, what can I do for you?"

The boy said, "Old Sage, they tell me that you can give me the secret of happiness and success in life. I want to know that secret."

After a moment the old sage stopped rocking—stood up—and

grasped the boy by the hand. He led the boy down the path to the edge of the lake. He didn't stop at the edge of the water, but continued right on into it.

The water was soon up to the lad's knees—then his chest and shoulders—and finally over the boy's head. The old sage held the boy submerged in the water for what seemed to the boy a tremendous length of time. Finally they turned around and made their way back out of the water, up the path and back to the cabin.

The old sage sat down in his rocking chair and began to rock to and fro. Then he looked at the boy and said, "Lad, what did you want more than anything else in the world when you were under the water?"

The boy answered quickly, "A breath of air." The old sage said, "Lad, when you are determined to find success in life as badly as you wanted that breath of air, you will have found the secret."

This thought can apply to many of us—sometimes we dream of great achievements, great success, but you know, OFTEN WE DON'T KNOW WHAT IT IS WE REALLY WANT. We must DECIDE what we really want from life and when we want it badly enough and have the COURAGE and DETERMINATION to go after it, we'll achieve it.

I read and memorized the following words of Professor William James, the father of modern psychology from Harvard. I encourage you to read, reread and memorize this and repeat it often.

"Let no youth have any anxiety about the upshot of his education, whatever the line of it may be. If he keeps faithfully busy each hour of the working day, he may safely leave the final result to itself. He can, with perfect certainty, count on waking up some fine morning to find himself one of the competent ones of his generation, in whatever pursuit he may have singled out."

We have these words for strength and hope from one of the greatest, well-known psychologists in the world. Do the things suggested in this book, practice, improve—DON'T GIVE UP and "Your Time" will come. SELL YOURSELF ON YOURSELF AND ON YOUR POTENTIAL. Be determined to be a true professional in your field. Be determined to get desired, QUALITY RESULTS. That's a Pro—Make that decision today, Now! Have a BURNING DESIRE to CREATE your bright future. No one is stopping you but you! REALIZE THAT LACK OF COURAGE GUARANTEES FAILURE!!

Emerson said: "He has not learned the lesson of life who does not every day surmount a fear." He further stated: "Fear always springs from ignorance. Men suffer all their life long under the foolish superstition that they can be cheated. But it is as impossible for a man to be cheated by anyone but himself as for a thing to be and not to be at the same time."

We actually cheat ourselves of the truly great, successful life that we could know because we do not have the courage. We're afraid to try.

Picture in your mind the thing that you have decided you want from life . . . want it badly enough and go after it *immediately* with bold courage and conviction. It will be yours!

▲ ▲ ▲ ▲

"GARDLINES" *by Grant G. Gard*

DON'T TALK ABOUT THESE THINGS—DO THEM NOW!!

1. DECIDE what you want from life.
2. Prepare yourself to CAPITALIZE ON OPPORTUNITIES that come.
3. Don't let ADVERSITIES stand in your way.

4. Have the COURAGE and DETERMINATION to bring about "YOUR TIME."
5. Realize God has equipped you with the necessary tools to become the type of person that you really want to become and to do the things with your life that you really want to do.
6. Read something daily, listen to tapes, and attend anything educational to really prepare yourself. PRACTICE WHAT YOU LEARN.
7. Become the "Most competent one of your generation."
8. BELIEVE you can SUCCEED and do the things necessary to bring about your SUCCESS.
9. NEVER give up!
10. Be DETERMINED to make yourself a real "Pro."
11. Have a BURNING DESIRE to CREATE your bright future.
12. PICTURE IN YOUR MIND the thing you have decided you really want from life.
13. Be determined to FIND A WAY, don't make up excuses.
14. Drop membership in the "IF ONLY" Club IMMEDIATELY!
15. Think only in terms of "CANS" . . . not "CAN NOTS."
16. Have a STRONG PURPOSE in life.
17. NEVER get down on YOURSELF.

▲ ▲ ▲ ▲

THOUGHT PROVOKING QUOTES

"A wise man will make more opportunities than he finds.
—*Bacon*

"Every mistake is an opportunity for learning."
—*Ralph Waldo Emerson*

"There are no difficulties in life; there are only opportunities."
—*C. V. Thomas*

"Readiness for opportunity makes for success. Opportunity often comes by accident; readiness never does."
—*Samuel Rayburn*

"The surest way not to fail is to determine to succeed."
                                                    —*Sheridan*

"There is no education like adversity."
                                                    —*Disraeli*

"We are living in a world of permanent change. A person is constantly called upon to create his own future."
                                                    —*Gregory Brown*

"Do what you feel in your heart to be right—for you'll be criticized anyway. You'll be damned if you do and damned if you don't."
                                                    —*Eleanor Roosevelt*

"He that loses money loses little, he that loses health loses much, but he that loses courage loses all."
                                                    —*Anonymous*

"Perhaps there is no more important component of character than steadfast resolution. The boy who is going to make a great man, or is going to count in any way in afterlife, must make up his mind not merely to overcome a thousand obstacles, but to win in spite of a thousand repulses and defeats."
                                                    —*Theodore Roosevelt*

"Impossible is a word to be found in the dictionary of fools."
                                                    —*Napoleon*

"No man ever became great or good except through many and great mistakes."
                                                    —*William Gladstone*

"Ask and it shall be given you; seek and ye shall find; knock and it shall be opened unto you."
                                                    —*Matthew 7:7*

"All things, whatsoever ye shall ask in prayer, believing, ye shall receive."
                                                    —*Matthew 21:22*

"No one can make you feel inferior without your consent."
                                                    —*Eleanor Roosevelt*

2 | *Paving the Road to Your Full Potential*

The A-K-A-W Formula. If at any time in the future or right now, we are not making the progress we want on our jobs or in our home life, it's because our attitude is off; we don't fully understand what we are doing; we don't know how to apply knowledge; or we aren't working wisely. I call it the A-K-A-W formula, the 4 checking points of success and happiness.

    A = Attitude
    K = Knowledge
    A = Application of Knowledge
    W = Working Wisely

STINKIN' THINKIN'—MENTAL HALITOSIS

Attitude. There is very little difference in people, but that little difference makes a big difference! The LITTLE difference is ATTITUDE. The BIG difference is whether it is Positive or

Negative. We must accept that we can have knowledge, we can apply our knowledge correctly and be working wisely, but with "STINKIN' THINKIN' or MENTAL HALITOSIS" for an ATTI-TUDE, it's all in vain. ATTITUDE is the most important of the four areas because it determines everything we do in life and to the degree that we get things accomplished. Without the right type of ATTITUDE we are filled with self-doubt and fear. I am convinced that self-doubt and fear defeat more people today by depriving them from living a happy life and accomplishing their goals than any other reasons.

I have spoken to hundreds of conventions, company and professional meetings, men and women from all walks of life, and in practically every group there are the *doubters* that certain ideas, services, concepts, or products can be put across successful-ly, while others are doing that very thing successfully. What's the difference? ATTITUDE! What will drive one person on to greater heights will be the kiss of death for the next person.

Nothing can stop the person who is filled with the right type of ATTITUDE from achieving his goals. The type of person filled with the wrong attitude? Sorry, nothing is going to help that person. Check your attitude. JOBS DON'T HAVE FUTURES, PEOPLE DO AND IT'S OUR ATTITUDE THAT WILL DETERMINE OUR FUTURE.

Knowledge. Complete knowledge of the things we are doing is a must if we are going to be confident; win the confidence of others; build a good self-image of ourselves (poor self-image and everything else is wrong); and create a favorable image for our profession, industry, company and the people we are attempting to influence.

This is the day of PROFESSIONALISM, the day of SPE-CIALIZATION. We must EARN THE RIGHT to do the thing we are doing and that means know ten to twenty times as much about our idea, concept or service as we can use when we are influencing others to our way of thinking.

But do not fall under the notion that knowledge is power. It is not!! You can have a head full of the best ideas, concepts, products, and services and they can be the best kept secret in America if you are not able to relate them to people and situations effectively.

Recently, I was visiting with the training director of a large insurance company. This man told me, "Grant, you can be a walking actuary, a walking encyclopedia, know all the facts, figures, interest charts, annuities and events and starve to death in this business. We have thousands of guys doing it every day. They can't sell insurance for sour apples."

Why do they fail to obtain desired results? Because they forget that they are in the PEOPLE BUSINESS and they cannot relate their knowledge effectively to PEOPLE and PEOPLE PROBLEMS.

In conversation with the President of a large milling company, I inquired of him, "How do you possibly determine who is going to get a promotion with all of the highly-skilled and technical people you have in your employ?" He replied, "Of course, we have highly technical people in our plant. They have to have a great amount of technical knowledge or we wouldn't have hired them in the first place. We can get all the people that we want with great amounts of technical knowledge from any university or college. But the person who gets the promotion in our plant is the one who knows how to *relate his knowledge* to people and the one who *works smoothly with others.*"

It's possible, then, to have lots of knowledge and still have very little education, and, on the other hand, it's possible to have a great deal of education and still have very little knowledge. You and I know of many people who have great amounts of both knowledge and education and still fail to be effective in dealing with people and situations. They just cannot relate to people and situations effectively.

Know all that you possibly can about the thing that YOU are doing and you will build confidence in yourself and win the confidence of others.

Application of Knowledge. That's where the power is. It's our ability to APPLY OUR KNOWLEDGE to people and situations to obtain desired results. We must be able to motivate people into positive action with our KNOWLEDGE. Our success depends on our ability to attract and influence people to obtain desired results. We must be able to do two things with the knowledge that we have. . . . We must be able to COMMUNICATE with it effectively and we must be able to MOTIVE with it effectively.

During a practice session for the Green Bay Packers when things were not going well for Vince Lombardi's team, Lombardi singled out one big guard for his failure to "put out." It was a hot, muggy day when the coach called his guard aside and leveled his awesome vocal guns on him, as only Lombardi could, "Son, you are a lousy football player. You're not blocking, you're not tackling, you're not putting out. As a matter of fact, it's all over for you today, go take a shower." The big guard dropped his head and walked into the dressing room. Forty-five minutes later, when Lombardi walked in, he saw the big guard sitting in front of his locker still wearing his uniform. His head was bowed and he was sobbing quietly.

Vince Lombardi, ever the changeable but always the compassionate warrior, did something of an about face that was also typical of him. He walked over to his football player and put his arm around his shoulder. "Son," he said, "I told you the truth. You are a lousy football player. You're not blocking, you're not tackling, you're not putting out. However, in all fairness to you, I should have finished the story. Because inside of you, son, there is a great football player and I'm going to stick by your side until the great football player inside of you has a chance to come out and assert himself.''

With these words, Jerry Kramer straightened up and felt a great deal better. As a matter of fact, he felt so much better that he went on to become one of the all-time greats in football and was recently voted the all-time guard in the first 50 years of professional football.

The "Pro" leader must be able to communicate his ideas to people and motivate people to peak performance so that he gets maximum production from his people.

The "Pro" salesperson must be able to communicate with prospects and motivate prospects into positive action to get maximum results from his time and territory.

The real "Pro" community leader must be able to communicate with members of the church, school, or community and motivate them into "Making things happen" and into "Keeping things moving."

Yes, the PRO knows he must be a "People builder" as well as a "People mover" . . . moving people in a positive way to obtain desired results.

Work Wisely. You know and I know a lot of people who are good people, they mean well, they work hard, but they simply don't progress on their jobs and it's because they haven't learned the big difference in this statement: "We must do the RIGHT THINGS RIGHT instead of just doing THINGS RIGHT." We MUST learn to do the RIGHT THINGS RIGHT versus doing THINGS RIGHT if we are going to be happy and successful.

We can't afford to develop any bad habits. People who are doing things right just go around in circles doing the same thing day in and day out, year in and year out, never trying to improve on the quality of their work. They can be doing the WRONG THINGS RIGHT (and most of them are) and be wasting all that precious time and energy. We must learn to do the RIGHT THINGS RIGHT with the RIGHT PERSON at the RIGHT TIME to obtain the RIGHT RESULTS.

MAKE A HABIT OF DOING THE RIGHT THINGS RIGHT

"The way to break a bad habit," says James T. Mangan, "is to undertake the FIRST abstinence. You may be smoking, drinking, or eating too much—and you admit it isn't good for you. How to stop? REFRAIN THIS ONCE! Now dwell on this single act of abstention. Isn't it a great experience? This self-satisfaction contains more joy than the indulgence itself. You are now aware that you CAN abstain; you are stronger and more skillful at coping with the next temptation. 'A kind of easiness' has been given you for the next battle, and your heart has come to know that there is more pleasure in destroying a bad habit than in preserving it."

Analyze yourself and BREAK BAD HABITS IMMEDIATELY. It's only when we analyze ourselves and become aware of our strengths and weaknesses do we grow.

How do you measure a person? There's only one way and that's by the *desirable results* achieved, by performances, by track records and by accomplishments.

By sharpening these four areas—A/K/A/W—you'll achieve even more, improve your performance and make a better "track" for yourself.

WHEN THE MAN IS RIGHT, THE WORLD IS RIGHT

A young minister was taking care of his small son while his wife was away. He thought he would prepare his sermon for the next Sunday but his young son had other ideas. As youngsters will do, he began to disturb the minister by getting into everything available and by asking his father many questions. Finally when the father's patience was exhausted, he went to his files and discovered a map of the world.

Together they cut the map into small pieces like a jigsaw puzzle. The father gave the puzzle to the boy to put the picture back together and asked the boy to come back and get him just as soon as he had finished putting the map back together. The young minister went back to his study and in a very short time, possibly twenty or thirty minutes, he heard a knock on his door. There was the youngster, full of excitement and ready to show his dad the results of his work. They made their way back to the kitchen and sure enough, the world was again in its original form.

The father said, "Son, how did you ever get that map back together so fast?" The boy said, "Daddy, I looked at it and found on the other side that there was a picture of a man—so I put the man together and then turned it over. I found that when THE MAN WAS RIGHT, THE WORLD WAS RIGHT."

And so it is with our own mental attitude. If we allow ourselves to think negatively, many times it appears that the world is against us, but when we develop the "I CAN AND WILL DO IT" attitude; when we develop the habit of positive thinking; when we get OURSELVES RIGHT, we usually find that the WORLD IS RIGHT.

POSITIVE ATTITUDE + INTEGRITY = A WINNER

One of the traits that made Harry S. Truman a great man was his INTEGRITY. Nowhere was this better demonstrated than in the autumn of 1948. He was at the time campaigning for reelection against a powerful opponent, Thomas E. Dewey of New York.

No one gave Truman much chance to win. The public opinion polls showed Dewey far ahead. Southern Democrats had put up their own candidate, and many northern Democrats were backing still another. Worst of all, little money was coming in for the President's campaign. There was danger that radio speeches which he had planned would have to be canceled because of lack of funds with which to pay the networks.

At this dark moment the President held a meeting with a small group of advisors and asked for their frank opinions on the situation. Without exception, they expressed grave doubt and gloom. Mr. Truman listened attentively, smiled to show that he had not taken their candor amiss, and said, "Oh, now, I don't think it's that bad."

Someone said, "But, Mr. President, you can't run a campaign without money."

"Who said so?" the President retorted. "We're doing it, aren't we?"

He was interrupted by a telephone call from a wealthy man who was known to be a big contributor to political campaigns. Rumor had reached him, said this millionaire, that the Democratic Party needed $20,000 in a hurry to pay for radio time, and he was willing to put up the cash—but he hinted that in return he would expect Mr. Truman to carry out certain policies if he were elected. In a clear, firm voice the President said, "You can contribute your money or you can keep it, but I'm not making any deals!" Then he hung up.

This response—the response of a man of courage and integrity—had an electrifying effect on his staff. Suddenly their own morale and hopes revived. They threw themselves into their tasks with renewed zeal. The next day the President received a call from another man of wealth, who said, "Mr. President, I've just heard what you told So-and-So" (referring to the previous caller).

"You're the kind of man the country needs in the White House. I'm sending in a campaign contribution—twenty thousand—and I'm going after my friends to make them do likewise—and no strings attached."

The needed money began to roll in, the campaign reached new heights of enthusiasm, the American people responded to Mr. Truman's fighting spirit, and he scored one of the most startling upsets in American political history.

A positive attitude and integrity always makes a WINNER.

DON'T STOP—GO TO THE TOP

A group of sportsmen met in a small inn at the foot of the majestic Alps in Switzerland to hear a noted mountain climber and Alpine guide speak about his experiences as a climber of mountains.

During his talk many of the men became enthusiastic about mountain climbing. So after the talk they approached the speaker and asked him if he would guide them on their very own climb the following day. He said he would, so they gathered all of their gear and supplies together and met early the next morning to start climbing the mountain.

They climbed for several hours and finally arrived at a cabin halfway up the side of the mountain. This was a place to stop to get warm and refresh themselves before they continued their ascent to the top. They built a fire and brewed a pot of coffee and settled back to relax for a short time. Soon one of the climbers came to the guide and said, "You know, my ankle is sore from an old injury, and I'm afraid if I continue on I may have a lot of trouble with it. If it's O.K. with you I'll wait here and join the rest of you on the way down."

Soon another climber, who had a sore foot, asked if he could be excused and he, too, would join the party on the way back down. One after one some of the others gave one excuse or another until there was only a handful left to go on to the top of the hill. The rest remained at the halfway house. In a short time the remaining climbers began the rest of the climb to the top.

About the middle of the day, one of the men who had remained at the halfway house was gazing out the window up toward the top of the mountain when suddenly he said, "Hey, fellows, look up there. There's Tom . . . there's Bill . . . there are the rest of them. They're going all the way to the top. They all made it all the way to the top."

This is the way it is with so many people in life. So many of us make a good start but the going gets tough and then we stop at the halfway house. It seems that often we're not willing to keep climbing . . . we're not willing to pay the price of SUCCESS . . . we'd rather make up some EXCUSE that sounds good and remain at the halfway house while others go right on up to the top. When the going gets tough—that's when the tough get going!

DON'T LET ANYONE OR ANYTHING STOP YOU

Regardless of the past, be it good or bad, and the uncertainties of the tomorrows, NO ONE CAN ACCOMPLISH ANYTHING GREATER THAN THAT WHICH HE REALLY IS.

It is indeed a great tragedy to see and hear top management people crying for qualified people to fill important jobs and so many people doing absolutely nothing to further improve themselves so they can improve their lifes' circumstances.

Having been in the business world and the self-improvement business for 25 years, I have talked to many top management people about training for their personnel. Top management wants their people to spend time in personal development programs because they know that production goes up with better trained supervisors and sales go up with better trained salespeople.

In a good many cases, companies pay part and sometimes all of the tuition to find that about only 10–20% of their people have the right type of attitude and are interested enough in their jobs and their futures to spend the effort and a little of their money improving themselves to do an even better job and to place themselves in line for promotion or for higher income. YOUR REWARDS IN LIFE COME AS A DIRECT RESULT AS TO HOW VALUABLE A PERSON YOU BECOME. The scales always balance out. Your future depends upon your FUTURE EARNING POWER and how good, how efficient, and how valuable you make yourself.

A Texan bought a young horse that he felt had the potential of becoming a real winner. He had the best jockey that money would buy and managed to obtain an excellent trainer. Every day the trainer and the jockey would work with the horse developing his potential and seeing to it that he was fed properly. And sure enough, in a short period of time, the horse proved to be a real winner. He won his first big purse and the Texan built a corral along the side of the highway and erected a large sign which read, "Here's the fastest race horse the world has ever seen."

The Texan discontinued the good training and feeding habits of the horse, trying to rest on his laurels. One day, another man came by and challenged the Texan's horse to a race with his horse. This time the Texan's horse came in last. The Texan had to change the sign to read, "Here's the fastest world this race horse has ever seen."

Daily personal development is a real MUST if we are going to progress in our profession.

Top management is the first to tell you that 80–90% of the promotions come from those 10–20% who do take advantage of some type of self-improvement training program.

Working with company management where there were 15 salespeople present, plus the boss, I was told that the boss would like to see every one of his salespeople attend a seminar that was to cost $29.50 per person. He said that, as a test, he wanted to see how many of the 15 would go ahead on their own and spend their own time and money without the company paying any of the tuition since they should realize that they are straight commission salespeople and the more they sell, the more they make.

The boss encouraged his people to attend without mentioning that the company would pay 50% of the tuition. On that basis, two people purchased tickets! He then mentioned that the company would pay 50% or one-half and then seven more bought tickets. But six out of the 15 would not attend regardless of what the boss did. Any wonder that the persons who improve themselves with the A-K-A-W formula get ahead so rapidly?

I heard the President of a company explain to his managers and supervisors that he would like them to attend a self-development workshop in the near future. The President stated that he would reimburse 50% of a $38.00 ticket after attendance at the workshop. There were 40 managers and supervisors present. The boss said, "No more paying 100% in advance . . . the last time I did that quite a number of you didn't show up at the workshop, so this time first you go, and then we'll reimburse you 50%." Twelve purchased tickets! Can you imagine how the President of that company must have felt . . . first to pay 100% and have some managers and supervisors so uninterested in their work that they would not even attend after the company paid 100% and then to find that 12 out of 40 is all that would attend on a 50% reimbursement basis? How would you feel if you were the boss?

I visited recently with the Executive Vice President of a bank and asked him what percent of his employees attended self-improvement programs that would make them more valuable on the job. His answer—"I'd be lucky to get 10–15% to attend even if I paid the entire tuition!"

COMPETITION IS KEEN IN ANY FIELD. Industry and companies are trying to do everything they can to HELP their people increase sales; to make people more productive; to create a better image; and to meet and beat competition and to CREATE COMPETITION only to have such a high number of people not willing to improve their lot in life.

I congratulate you on reading this book. Do something everyday to help yourself CREATE your favorable circumstances for the future because YOU CAN NEVER ACCOMPLISH ANYTHING GREATER THAN THAT WHICH YOU REALLY ARE!!

The best always rise to the top!! Like the old bottle of milk we used to get . . . you could shake it and the milk and cream would mix, but let it sit for a few minutes and they would separate with the cream going to the top. You can rest assured that those who are the creators of their favorable circumstances will eventually rise to the top.

TWO TYPES OF PEOPLE

Since the beginning of my career in self-improvement, I have noticed there are two distinct types of people. About 80% to 90% of the people in this country just want a job, no particular challenge, no stress on their capabilities, just happy and content to do the same thing day in and day out. Then, there is the 10% to 20% group who do something part or all of the time to enable themselves to accept more responsibilities to solve bigger problems and challenges and to meet difficulties head on.

I heard the pastor of one of the largest Baptist churches in

Lubbock, Texas, give his farewell address to a service club to which he belonged. He was being transferred to Kansas to accept an even larger church. He said that he got the topic for that day as a result of a question that had been asked him a few days before: "What do you consider the biggest problem leaders face today?" His answer and talk was on "People Will Not Accept Responsibility—People Have Excusitus."

I knew a man on the Union Pacific Railroad in my little home town of Overton, Nebraska, who worked as a section hand. He had worked for about 20 years prior to the day I was visiting with him back in about 1950. I asked him that day if he had any regrets working for the railroad. His reply: "My biggest regret was that a few years ago I was offered a promotion to road master and I turned it down. I really didn't want to accept the additional responsibilities. I guess I didn't have the courage and confidence to accept." Then he said, "I NEVER GOT THE SECOND CHANCE."

He is now retired and retired on the same level he was on at the time he started his career. You and I know lots of people like that. They make up excuses to cover up the real reasons that they don't accept more responsibility. Excuses like: "I don't know how." "I don't have the time." "My car needs gas." "My work load is too heavy now." In reality what they are really saying is: "I am afraid." "I don't have the self-confidence." "I doubt that it can be done that way." These people are real "SELF-DOUBTERS." These people have a POOR SELF-IMAGE, and lack REAL DESIRE to make a success of their lives.

Too few people do things to help themselves grow, become more skilled and confident, and have a deep down DESIRE to better themselves and their positions in life. They live in a WORLD OF SELF-PITY and don't do the things necessary to bring about favorable results.

"CHECK UP" BEFORE YOU "CHECK OUT"

The time has come for us to stop and take a look at ourselves and see how we are doing. A young man in a drugstore phone booth . . . he had left the door of the booth ajar so the druggist couldn't help overhearing his conversation. "I want to talk to the boss" was his opening gambit. "Please connect me. This is the boss? Well, how would you like to hire a new on-his-toes office boy? . . . You already have one who is entirely satisfactory? No way to persuade you to make a change? O.K., I'm sorry. Thanks anyhow for listening to me. Goodbye."

After the young man hung up the druggist told him, "I couldn't help hearing what you said over the phone just now. I like your initiative and I'm sorry you didn't connect on that job. Better luck next time."

"Thanks," said the young man airily, "BUT EVERYTHING IS JUST DANDY. THAT WAS MY OWN BOSS I WAS TALKING TO. I WAS JUST DOING A LITTLE CHECKING UP ON MYSELF."

Check up on yourself and refuse to "make up excuses," and make sure your SELF-IMAGE is good and you have REAL DESIRE to move ahead.

EARN MORE THAN YOU RECEIVE

At a monthly meeting of the Board of Trustees of a small rural church, there was talk of giving the pastor a long-delayed raise in pay. When the idea was suggested to the pastor, he declined.

"Gentlemen," he said, "I don't want you to raise my salary any more. I'm having too much trouble collecting what you're already paying me!"

You always get back what you send out. WHAT'S AROUND YOU IS YOU. Make yourself so valuable you don't have trouble collecting pay for your services. The scales always balance out. *Your income is the measure of your service to others.*

PEOPLE WON'T CARE ABOUT YOU UNTIL THEY FIRST KNOW HOW MUCH YOU CARE ABOUT THEM

To succeed in any profession you must have a "SERVICE" attitude or "BENEFIT" attitude toward people as your primary goal at all times, then success is assured. Community leaders, management personnel, salespeople, employees and parents can read books, take courses of every type, but NO ONE CAN FORGET THIS VERY IMPORTANT FACT—In the long run, NO TECHNIQUES, regardless of how clever they are, can conceal the REAL MOTIVES people have in their hearts. THE RIGHT MOTIVES ARE EVEN MORE IMPORTANT THAN THE RIGHT MOVES.

What do people value most in a leader, manager, salesperson, or parent? The majority of us want someone who is honest, truthful and straight-forward, someone we really know who has OUR TRUE INTEREST at heart, someone we can trust.

To give real service you must add something which cannot be bought or measured with money—SINCERITY AND INTEGRITY. This is something that cannot be faked, at least not for long. If you have the best interests of your people at heart, it will show in your actions time and time again. You'll build a reservoir of goodwill.

Unfortunately, sometimes leaders, salespeople, and parents aren't all that concerned about the welfare of their people, but they only want to use and manipulate them. No matter how glib such people are, or how clever as amateur psychologists, their motives will show through. They are bound to!

No leader can create a feeling of mutual trust with people

overnight. It takes time and effort . . . Nor can sincerity be turned on and off like a light. Leaders who are insincere don't have to advertise the fact—it's visible in everything they do and it soon becomes common knowledge to everyone. Likewise, insincerity cannot be hidden, disguised or covered up no matter how competent a leader may otherwise be.

The only way to keep the goodwill and high esteem of the people you are working with is to DESERVE IT. No one can fool all the people all the time. Each of us, eventually, is recognized for exactly what we are—not what we appear to be. Your FUTURE is determined, therefore, by your PRESENT THOUGHT PATTERN and the ATTITUDE you now hold about yourself, your profession, your boss, your family, your products and services, your employees, your associates and others.

It's all in how you view things, the type of mental pictures you have about new challenges, about growing with self-improvement, what kind of a person you see yourself being. Your experiences today are not caused by yesterday, but are an out-picturing of your present mental thought pictures . . . CHANGE YOUR THOUGHT PICTURES NOW AND YOU CHANGE EVERYTHING NOW. DON'T TALK ABOUT IT—DO IT NOW!

YOUR MENTAL ATTITUDE IS YOUR REAL BOSS

Two shoe salesmen went to Africa to open up new territories. Three days after their arrival, the first salesman sent a cable to his office, "Returning next plane, can't sell shoes here, everybody goes barefoot."

Nothing was heard from the other salesman for about two weeks. Then came a fat air mail letter with this message for the home office, "Fifty orders enclosed. Prospects unlimited. Nobody here has shoes."

The difficult challenges quickly bring to surface the thinking pattern of the TOP-NOTCH PERSON, THE DOER, versus the MEDIOCRE or FAILURE. Simply stated, YOUR MENTAL ATTITUDE IS YOUR REAL BOSS.

Read these inspirational words from Ralph Waldo Emerson . . .

"There is a time in every man's education when he arrives at the conviction that envy is ignorance, that imitation is suicide; that he must take himself for better or for worse as his portion; that though the wide universe is full of good, no kernel of nourishing corn can come to him but through his toil bestowed on that plot of ground which is given to him to till. The power which resides in him is new in nature, and none but he knows what that is which he can do, nor does he know until he had tried . . .

Trust thyself; every heart vibrates to that iron string. Accept the place the divine providence has found for you, the society of your contemporaries, the connection of events. Great men have always done so . . .

My life is for itself and not for a spectacle. I much prefer that it should be of a lower strain, so it be genuine and equal, than that it should be glittering and unsteady . . . Few men and mean as my gifts may be, I actually am, and do not need for my own assurance or the assurance of my fellows any secondary testimony.

What I must do is all that concerns me, not what the people think. This rule, equally arduous in actual and in intellectual life, may serve, for the whole distinction between greatness and meanness. It is the harder because you will always find those who think they know what is your duty better than you know it. It is easy in the world to live after the world's opinion; it is easy in solitude to live after your own; but the great man is he who in the midst of the crowd keeps with perfect sweetness the independence of solitude."

Don't let anyone or anything stop you from realizing your full potential. Trust yourself, your judgment and till your plot of ground every day planting only courageous, resourceful and positive result mind pictures.

Remember, everything is determined by your ATTITUDE, IDEAS and YOUR PRESENT THOUGHTS. Use the laws of the mind to greater achievement and create your own bright circumstances. Living in this wonderful, free enterprise country with potential unlimited, there can be only one thing in the world holding you back and that is yourself!

ACCEPT NEW AND BIGGER CHALLENGES

This book is intended to give you new ideas to help you mentally shape your attitude. It is intended to help you have a HEALTHY, POSITIVE ATTITUDE, more PEOPLE, LEADER-SHIP, SALES and JOB KNOWLEDGE along with additional SKILLS to enable you to WORK WISELY, so that you will be better equipped to accept and go after bigger challenges in life! These areas will be covered in the following chapters.

▲ ▲ ▲ ▲

"GARDLINES" *by Grant G. Gard*

DON'T TALK ABOUT THESE THINGS—DO THEM NOW!!

1. Evaluate yourself as honestly as possible as to the four major check areas, A-K-A-W. Ask yourself, "How is my ATTI-TUDE?" "Do I really have the KNOWLEDGE to do my job successfully?" "Am I APPLYING MY KNOWLEDGE correctly to all types of situations, and am I WORKING WISELY?" (Might be a good idea to ask your wife, husband, or boss to give you

an honest evaluation—Many times we don't see ourselves as other people see us.)

2. Be determined not to have "STINKIN' THINKIN'".
3. Have a HEALTHY, POSITIVE ATTITUDE.
4. BE RIGHT WITH THE WORLD. When the man is right, the world is right.
5. Be determined to pay the price of success and NEVER QUIT until you get what you started after.
6. Be determined to NEVER STOP AT THE HALF WAY POINT . . . don't be a quitter.
7. CREATE your circumstances through "Growing with challenges" and by forming the "Right type mind pictures NOW".
8. DON'T RUN from responsibility.
9. TRUST YOURSELF AND YOUR JUDGMENT and do not be governed by what others might say about you.
10. Be SERVICE and BENEFIT MINDED at all times realizing that's the only way you can reach true success.
11. Be known as "THE ONE WHO GETS THINGS DONE"!
12. BREAK BAD HABITS immediately.
13. Increase your FUTURE EARNING POWER by becoming more valuable.
14. Apply SINCERITY and INTEGRITY to all situations.
15. EARN more than you receive. Things always balance out.
16. Always have a GOOD SELF-IMAGE. Don't be a "Self-Doubter".

▲　▲　▲　▲

THOUGHT PROVOKING QUOTES

"There's nothing either good or bad but thinking makes it so."
—Shakespeare

"It isn't the size of the dog in a fight, but the size of the fight in the dog."
—Tom Barrett

"Success or failure in business is caused more by mental attitude even than by mental capacities."

—Walter Dill Scott

"All that a man achieves and all that he fails to achieve is the direct result of his own thoughts."

—James Allen

"Do the thing you fear to do and the death of fear is certain."
—Ralph Waldo Emerson

"Our greatest glory is not in never falling but in rising everytime we fall."

—Confucius

"If God be with us, who can be against us?"
—Romans 8:31

"Without faith a man can do nothing, with it all things are possible."
—Sir William Osler

"The elevator to success has been out of order—Sorry, you'll have to take the stairway—one step at a time."

—Unknown

"The world stands aside to let anyone pass who knows where he is going."

—David Starr Jordon

"Much good work is lost for the lack of a little more."
—E. H. Harriman

"Be true to your own highest convictions."
—William E. Channing

"All that a man does outwardly is but the expression and completion of his inward thought. To work effectively, he must think clearly; to act nobly, he must think nobly.

—William E. Channing

"He who adds not to his learning diminishes it."
—The Talmud

3 | *The Winning Attitude*

To Win Is Everything. How many times in life have we heard the old cliche, "IT DOESN'T MATTER WHETHER WE WIN OR LOSE, IT'S ALL IN HOW WE PLAY THE GAME?" This, among many other negative cliches, provides us with a pacifier when we don't produce desired results.

To any person who has ever been successful, it makes one whale of a difference whether one wins or loses. PEOPLE LIKE TO WORK FOR AND DO BUSINESS WITH WINNERS!! Turnover is high among losers. Losers go from one job to another thinking that it is the job instead of themselves.

If you don't think it makes any difference whether you win or lose, have a conversation with a football, basketball, or baseball coach who has just had a losing season. People do not like to pay to see losers. People flock to games and really support a winning team. WINNING IS EVERYTHING!

People like to do business with and work for "winners" just as they will enthusiastically support a winning team. God forbid, the person who doesn't take his or her profession or job any more seriously than to say, "It doesn't make any difference whether I got desired results or not, I sure played the game well."

WIN YOUR PLACE ON THE FIRST TEAM

Lou Little gained fame as a football coach at Columbia University. Before that, however, he coached at Georgetown in Washington, D.C. One year there was a youngster on the squad who was no great shakes as a football player, but whose personality served as a morale booster for the whole team. Little was deeply fond of the boy. He liked the proud way he walked arm in arm with his father on the campus from time to time. If the team was far enough ahead, the coach let him get into a game occasionally for the last few minutes of play.

One day, about a week before the big finale with Fordham, the boy's mother called Little on the phone. "My husband died this morning of a heart attack," she said. "Will you break the news to my boy? He'll take it better if it comes from you." Little did what was necessary, and the boy went home sorrowfully.

He was back three days later and came straight to Little. "Coach," he begged, "I want to ask something of you that means an awfully lot to me. I want to start in that game against Fordham. I think it's what my father would have liked most."

Little hesitated, and then agreed. "O.K., son, you'll start, but you'll only be in there for a play or two. You aren't quite good enough and we both know it." True to his word, Little started the boy—but never took him out. For sixty full, jarring minutes he played inspired football, running, blocking and passing like an All-American and sparking the team to victory.

Back in the clubhouse, Little threw his arm around the boy's shoulder and said, "Son, you were terrific today. You stayed in because you belonged there. You never played that kind of football before. What got into you?"

The boy answered, "Remember how my father and I used to go about arm in arm? There was something about him very few people knew. My father was totally blind. This afternoon was the first time he ever saw me play."

With the WINNING ATTITUDE and STRONG PURPOSE IN MIND, the boy went from a substitute to a first-rate player. You can move to a first-rate position in your profession with TRUE HEART POWER and WINNING ATTITUDE.

MEDIOCRITY—You can't promote it—You can't fire it—And you can't win with it.

TURN MINUSES INTO PLUSES

The young bride from the East who, during the last war, followed her husband to an Army camp on the edge of the desert in California. Living conditions were primitive at best and he had advised against it, but she wanted to be with him.

The only housing they could find was a run-down shack near an Indian village. The heat was unbearable in the daytime—115 degrees in the shade. The wind blew constantly, spreading dust and sand all over everything. The days were long and boring. Her only neighbors were the Indians, none of whom spoke English.

When her husband was ordered farther into the desert for two weeks of maneuvers, loneliness and the wretched living conditions got the best of her. She wrote to her mother that she was coming home—she just couldn't take any more. In a short time she received a reply which included these two lines:

Two men looked out from prison bars,

One saw mud, the other saw the stars.

She read the lines over and over and began to feel ashamed

of herself. And she didn't really want to leave her husband. All right, she'd LOOK for the stars.

In the following days she set out to make friends with the Indians. She asked them to teach her weaving and pottery. At first they were distant, but as soon as they sensed her interest was genuine they returned her friendship. She became fascinated with their culture, history—everything about them.

She began to study the desert as well, and soon it, too, changed from a desolate, forbidding place to a marvelous thing of beauty. She had her mother send her books. She studied the forms of the cacti, the yuccas and the Joshua trees. She collected seashells that had been left there millions of years ago when the sands had been an ocean floor. Later, she became such an expert on the area that she wrote a book about it.

What had changed? Not the desert; not the Indians. Simply by changing her own attitude she had transformed a miserable experience into a highly rewarding one.

You can change your miserable and negative experiences—the MINUSES—into very rewarding experiences—the PLUSES— simply by changing your attitude.

William James said, "The greatest discovery of my generation is that men can change their circumstances by changing their attitude of mind."

CHALLENGES ARE GOOD

Let's take a look and see what three people did with a WINNING ATTITUDE. These people had real problems or "challenges," but they succeeded in life and brought back their DESIRED RESULTS instead of wallowing in the world of SELF-PITY and EXCUSES.

In the first chair let's put a man who was paralyzed from his waist down and was confined to a wheelchair. He said to himself, "With a winning attitude I will win my challenge in life by doing something great for my country and will become the type of person that I want to become." You know who I'm talking about when I say that he was Governor of the state of New York and elected four times as President of the United States—Franklin Delano Roosevelt.

In the next chair let's put a man who was blind, but he said to himself, "This handicap isn't going to stop me from writing poetry. I will write poetry that will produce good mental images for people who have two good eyes." He wrote "Paradise Lost". I am referring to John Milton.

In the last chair let's place a man who was deaf and he said, "My handicap isn't going to stop me! I will write music that will be good listening for people who can hear." We listen to his music today. I am referring to Ludwig van Beethoven.

The question is—How would you respond to these challenges? Would you meet them head on and go through them as these men did or would you make up EXCUSES that sound good and be satisfied with your present situation in life? EVERY ADVERSITY CARRIES THE SEED TO GREATER ACHIEVEMENT IF WE JUST DON'T QUIT. A quitter never wins and a winner never quits!

Those ADVERSITIES helped to raise those people to new HEIGHTS. Your adversities can raise you to new heights with the right attitude. It takes a strong man to swim against the current—any dead fish will float with it!

PUT EXTRA EFFORT FORTH
WHEN THINGS LOOK THE WORST

A few years ago, I walked into my home in Colorado Springs, Colorado, and my son, David, a boy who had excelled in baseball, football and basketball, had a pair of gym trunks under his arm, even though, in his early years, he was told not to play in any type of sporting event because of a severe asthma condition. When I asked him where he was going, he said, "Dad, I needed a new challenge and the coach asked me to wrestle on the wrestling team."

I immediately said, "Dave, you shouldn't wrestle because you have braces on your teeth." This didn't stop him and the final payoff came when he was in the wrestling tournament.

I walked into the gym just as David started to wrestle his opponent. His opponent found out that David had braces on his teeth and he immediately went to work on his mouth. In the first two periods, the bout was stopped seven or eight times to repack David's mouth with gauze to stop the bleeding and at the end of the second round, David was behind eight points (8–0). I immediately went to the edge of the ring to stop the bout and started to bend over the ring when I heard the coach say, "Dave, you haven't lost the bout. However, the only way you can win this late in the match is to pin your man." Ten seconds after Period Three started, David had won the bout by pinning his man!

I cite this example for several reasons:

1. How would we respond after getting eight negative responses from people? Would we be able to turn eight minuses into one big plus?

2. When do you think that bout was actually won? When David got home that night, I asked him, "Dave, when did you decide that you could actually win that bout?" His reply, "THE FIRST DAY I WENT OUT FOR PRACTICE." Many times, before we ever enter into a situation, the outcome is determined before the event takes place.

3. THE WORST ADVICE WE EVER RECEIVE SOMETIMES COMES FROM THOSE WHO LOVE US THE MOST. I was going to stop that wrestling match because

I was fearful for my son. I did not know how much DEEP CONVICTION or BURNING DESIRE he really had to win that bout. Many times people offer us bad advice because they do not know OUR DESIRES, OUR DEEP CONVICTIONS to succeed at our endeavors. They are FEARFUL for us. This is really not hard to understand when we realize that 95% of the people are negative and only 5% are positive.

4. We can be very close to achieving our GOAL and still fail if we quit or give up too soon. We must see ourselves doing everything successfully and carrying out our projects successfully. WE ARE NOT WHAT WE THINK WE ARE, BUT WHAT WE THINK, WE ARE.

5. Apply extra effort when things are going badly and many times we can reverse the outcome and make it a POSITIVE EXPERIENCE.

We should have DESIRE, DETERMINATION AND DEDICATION, the three D's of a successful person. We must desire to "Win" and do the things necessary to bring this about starting right now—TODAY!

RESULTS OR EXCUSES

Unless people bring back DESIRED RESULTS, they are not going to stay in any profession very long. Few things are so embarrassing as watching someone do what you just said couldn't be done. We either produce RESULTS or we produce EXCUSES and there is no in between.

What's going to change if we stay in the same old pattern of making excuses? A tranquilizer that a lot of people take is something like this: "As soon as I've been in the business as long as old Charlie or Mollie, I'll be able to do what Charlie or Mollie can do." That's simply a TRANQUILIZER or EXCUSE for not producing desired results because years alone, in any profession, do not necessarily determine a person's success.

THE BUCK PASSING STOPS HERE

It was reported that President Harry Truman had a quote on his desk in the White House, "The Buck Stops Here". People should mentally quit passing the buck in the form of making up EXCUSES for BEING LOSERS. They should in turn have a WINNING ATTITUDE and be DETERMINED to overcome the CHALLENGES that are presented to them each day in every situation.

REACH FOR SOMETHING—DON'T RUN
FROM SOMETHING

With a winning attitude we can achieve our Great American Dream. That's the goal that we want to achieve for ourselves. I'm afraid that too many people are RUNNING FROM SOMETHING rather than REACHING FOR SOMETHING. Professional skill and a winning attitude give us the tools to use in making our goals a reality.

WHAT ARE YOU REALLY AFRAID OF? What is holding you back from reaching for something really big? Be thankful if you have a job that is a little harder than you like. A razor cannot be sharpened on a piece of velvet!

THE LOWEST EBB IS THE TURN OF THE TIDE

A young fellow who lived in the hill country liked to go to visit his girl friend. He would visit her two or three evenings a week if he could. The country was rough and, because he didn't have a horse, he had to walk quite a distance. He had to cross through the woods and across a canyon.

One evening he stayed a little longer than usual and when he started to leave he found that it was pitch dark. So he felt his way out to the road and started down the road staying as close to the middle as he could. He either had to make his way across the canyon or he could cross the railway trestle which would save him about a mile. So he pondered and finally decided to try the railroad trestle.

He felt his way carefully and slowly from one tie to the other and then he suddenly slipped and fell. Down and down he went, trying to grab hold of anything and finally he caught a brace. He hung on to the brace. His hands were bruised and his elbows were bruised. His face was scratched, but he had no choice—he had to hang on to the brace for dear life. He hung on all night and finally when dawn broke and when he could see, he found that he was only about two feet above the ground!

I believe that it was Henry Wadsworth Longfellow who said, "The lowest ebb is the turn of the tide." Probably all of us face dark periods in our lives and sometimes we feel like letting go, but if we have the COURAGE and CONFIDENCE to hold on a little longer, have a WINNING ATTITUDE, we usually find that things are not as bad as they seem.

I like the story of little Jimmie who just received a new pair of ice skates. He was out on the pond trying to learn how to skate, but he would fall and tumble more than skate. Finally a neighbor lady came over to Jimmie as he was trying to get up off the ice and said to him, "Jimmie, why don't you quit skating and go over to the side of the pond and watch the other kids skate?"

I love the little fellow's reply! He dried his tears and said,

"Ma'am, I didn't get these skates to learn to give up with . . . I got these skates to learn how with."

We better have that same attitude . . . learn how to do everything we can and as professionally as possible and never give up!

BE A DOER—NOT AN "AGINER"

Look at progress in a positive way, not in a negative way. For example, a 92-year old man who had lived in the same little town all of his life was told something like this: "I'll bet you've seen a lot of changes around here." He said, "*Yes Sir, and I've been dead set against every one of them.*"

He's the kind of a guy who is so negative that when he dies, he shouldn't be listed in the "Obituary Column . . . he should be under "Civic Improvement" . . . he's the kind of a guy who is so negative that he just brightens up a whole room when he leaves it.

Before the steamship was built, they said it could never be done. Then after the doers got it built, they said it would never be self-propelling. Then after they got it moving up the river, they said they could never get the darn thing stopped! While so many were saying it couldn't be done, there was a handful of doers who were ignoring them, bringing the steamship into reality.

The same thing was said about the airplane—that it couldn't be built, that it would never get off the ground! And once it was off the ground, they would never get it back on the ground. Always someone standing around being critical and saying that it just can't happen.

The real Pro says in reply to something like that, "I KNOW IT CAN'T BE DONE, BUT LET'S GO AHEAD AND DO IT ANYWAY." This is the person with a winning attitude and professional skills who accounts for 80% OF THE RESULTS in this country today. It's amazing to me that with no one standing over us placing LIMITATIONS on us that the figures don't change year to year. They stay about the same, that is, 20% of the people are getting 80% of the results. That also means that 80% of the people are getting 20% of the results and that isn't very much. These figures have stayed the same for the last twenty-five years.

ATTITUDE IS CONTAGIOUS

We cannot hide our ATTITUDE. IT'S CONTAGIOUS. It transmits just like a radio signal and it's one of being a loser or a winner. If a lady would walk into a roomful of people and she had a baby with her, provided the baby was old enough to crawl or walk, that baby would instinctively know who LIKES HIM and who DISLIKES HIM. Some people he would go to and some people he would completely ignore. Adults are the same way. They can tell whether or not we like people and situations. A WINNING ATTITUDE is a must. To be a winner we must THINK, ACT and TALK like we have already WON.

▲　　▲　　▲　　▲

"Gardlines" *by Grant G. Gard*

DON'T TALK ABOUT THESE THINGS—DO THEM NOW!!

1. Assume the WINNING ATTITUDE.
2. Be determined NOT TO BE BRAINWASHED by the negative statement, "It doesn't matter whether I win or lose, it's all in how I play the game," or any other negative statement.
3. Meet challenges head-on with a WINNING ATTITUDE.
4. Be determined to stay in the ring until DESIRED RESULTS

are achieved. Don't give up and make up EXCUSES.

5. Show by your ACTIONS, APPEARANCE and SPEECH that you constantly radiate the right type of attitude to everyone around you.
6. Be determined to hang on longer during dark periods, knowing that with COURAGE and with a WINNING ATTITUDE you will come out a "WINNER."
7. Don't let "NO'S" get you down.
8. DON'T RUN from anything—REACH for something.
9. Keep "razor sharp"—Do BIG things.
10. Attack each day with AMBITION and DRIVE.
11. Go after your job with DESIRE, DETERMINATION and DEDICATION.

▲　▲　▲　▲

THOUGHT PROVOKING QUOTES

"Every noble work is at first impossible."
—Carlyle

"The recipe for perpetual ignorance is to be satisfied with your opinions and content with your knowledge."
—Elbert Hubbard

"It is easier to be critical than correct."
—Edward R. Murrow

"An optimist makes opportunities out of difficulties, a pessimist makes difficulties out of opportunities."
—Reginald B. Mansell

"The optimist says the bottle is half full, the pessimist says the bottle is half empty."
—Unknown

"Adversity introduces a man to himself."
—Unknown

"The world expects results. Don't tell others about the labor pains. Show them the baby."

—Arnold Glasow

"Hit the ball over the fence and you can take your time going around the bases."

—John W. Roper

"The worst men often give the best advice."
—Philip J. Bailey

"There is no point high enough that one can say, 'This is the peak.'"
—Jascha Heifetz

"Circumstances are the rulers of the weak; they are but the instruments of the wise."

—Samuel Lover

"No one ever would have crossed the ocean if he could have gotten off the ship in the storm."

—C. F. Kettering

"Difficulties are meant to rouse, not discourage."
—William E. Channing

"What is defeat? Nothing but education; nothing but the first step to something better."

—Wendell Phillips

"If you are not afraid to face the music, you may get to lead the band."

—Edwin H. Stuart

"One man with courage makes the majority."
—Andrew Jackson

"The big shots are only the little shots who keep shooting."
—Christopher Morley

4 | *Plotting Your Course for Achievement*

If You Don't Know Where You are Going—You Might Already Be There. Life begins when we have a goal and it's over when we don't have one. You are staying young when you have worthy goals and you are expending your thoughts and energies in achieving those goals. YOU ARE STAYING YOUNG WHEN YOU LOOK AT THE FUTURE AS THOUGH IT IS A BRIGHT SHINING STAR. One of the secrets that you must utilize in setting goals is to be able to use your IMAGINATION to CREATE and VISUALIZE in your mind the thing that you want to MAKE HAPPEN for yourself.

MAKE YOUR DREAMS COME TRUE

There was an old sculptor in Mexico who had a large piece of granite moved to his back yard. In the spring of the year he started working—chiseling and grinding away as the school boys and girls walked by his place and watched him work. In the fall of the year, he had finished his project and had CREATED the thing that he had VISUALIZED, a lovely lion made of granite. As the school children passed they looked in amazement and saw the lion, and one of them remarked to the old sculptor, "I didn't know there was a lion in there." The sculptor had used his IMAGINATION and had VISUALIZED the lion and had made his dream come true.

PUT GOALS IN—TAKE SUCCESS OUT

Houdini, the greatest of all magicians, when once asked about the rabbit trick, made the remark, "There is no trick in taking the rabbit from the hat . . . the real trick is getting him in there in the first place!"

The same principal applies to us. There is no MAGICAL TRICK to becoming successful on the outside. The real accomplishment comes from putting in the RIGHT THINGS ON THE INSIDE that will create real accomplishment and generate success. Everything we do starts within us . . . GOALS, a map to follow through life.

J. C. Penney expressed it very well when he said, "Give me a stock clerk with a goal and I will give you a man who will make history. Give me a man without a goal, and I will give you a stock clerk."

STAND OUT . . . BE IN THE TOP 5%

Far too many people follow the path of least resistance and end up following the 95% of the people who do not set goals and who are just "walking motion," getting by in life the best they can with the least amount of effort. They are busy, they put in their hours and are very satisfied and comfortable in their own little "COMFORT ZONE". The man or woman with a goal is always busy making daily, weekly, monthly and yearly strides toward GREAT ACCOMPLISHMENTS . . . toward their GOALS.

There is a great amount of difference between being *busy with task* and being *busy with goals.* The person who is successful knows the bridge must be crossed from wishing to willing, from desiring to determining, from dreaming to doing, with the GOAL clearly in sight at all times.

John H. Fabre, the great French naturalist, conducted a most unusual experiment with some Processionary Caterpillars. These caterpillars blindly follow the caterpillar in front of them. Fabre carefully arranged them in a circle around the rim of a flower pot, so that the lead caterpillar actually touched the last caterpillar making a complete circle. In the center of the flower pot he placed some food. The caterpillars started around this circular flower pot. Around and around they went, hour after hour, day after day. After a week they started to drop off dead from exhaustion and starvation. With plenty of food less than six inches away, they literally starved to death because they kept busy following the caterpillar in front who obviously didn't know where he was going. They were so busy with *routine task* that they completely overlooked their goal or objective. Many people do a similar thing. They are busy with activities but a great amount of activities are MISGUIDED for lack of a goal.

PLOT YOUR EXACT COURSE

Everything in life starts with us as an INDIVIDUAL. Goals add PURPOSE and DIRECTION. Without goals we DRIFT. We are like a ship at sea with no rudder to guide it to its destination. When a ship leaves port it has its origin, sailing date, and it knows exactly what its destination is with the exact course it is going to take to get there, and the length of time it will take to arrive.

When you plan a trip you just don't walk in and say, "I want to buy an air line ticket". Immediately you would be asked, "From where and to where?" You would be given the time, dates, routing, etc. Most people spend more time planning trips and other activities than they do their goals in life. You can ask a captain of a ship or an airplane, "Where are we now?" And he can tell you exactly. How many of us could be asked, "Where are you now toward reaching your goal?" And give an exact reading?

Success is not a destination—it's a continuous journey fulfilling one achievement and then moving on to the next one, achieving one big overall worthy goal with our life. Success means different things to different people. To me it's the realization of a worthy achievement or goal. But the main thing is that we MUST KNOW WHAT THE GOAL IS!

I love to go pheasant hunting. In order to hit one, I have to see it, aim at it, and fire the gun. The same is true in life. We have to see our goals, aim at them and fire the energy and ammunition to hit them!

Here is a chart that will help YOU to greater personal achievement:

---

1. ESTIMATE AND EVALUATE YOUR PRESENT SIT-
   UATION
2. DEFINE AND SET REALISTIC, WORTHY AND
   DEFINITE GOALS
     a. Long Term
     b. Intermediate Term
     c. Short Term
3. WORK OUT A PLAN OF ACTION (What has to be
   done)

---

4. DETERMINE PROCEDURES (How it is to be done)
5. SET SCHEDULE FOR COMPLETION—DEADLINES
6. GET THE PLAN INTO ACTION WITHOUT PRO-CRASTINATION
7. CHART YOUR PROGRESS
8. KEEP YOUR GOALS IN FRONT OF YOU AT ALL TIMES
9. ALWAYS KEEP THINGS MOVING
10. NEVER LET UP
11. KEEP SETTING BIGGER GOALS AS DESIRED RE-SULTS ARE ACHIEVED

ZERO IN ON YOUR TARGET

Howard Hill was probably the greatest archer who ever walked on the face of this earth. He was so accurate and effective that he killed a bull elephant, a Bengal tiger, an African lion and a Cape Buffalo. They say that at 50 feet he could outshoot virtually any rifleman in the world. I have heard it said that not only could he always send an arrow in the center of the bull's eye, but also he could literally split that arrow with his next shot.

Howard Hill was a great man with a bow and arrow, BUT don't overlook one very important fact . . . HE COULD ALWAYS SEE HIS TARGET BEFORE HE SHOT THE ARROW!! You can't hit a target, a goal, if you don't have one—no more than you can come back from someplace you have never been.

In setting your goals, you should make careful RESEARCH and PLANNING as to the situation that now exists and, then going from that point to your REALISTIC LONG RANGE, INTERMEDIATE, and SHORT RANGE GOALS, and be very

SPECIFIC in DEFINING your goals.

Don't use general terms—Be specific—

DON'T USE	USE
A lot of money	$40,000 per year by (specific date)
A lovely home	A $75,000, 5-bedroom house, on 1 acre, paid for by (specific date)
Promotion	Executive V.P. by (specific date)
Read lots of books	Read 1 new book per week
Attend Seminars	Attend 1 Seminar every quarter
Vacation	A $1000, 2 week vacation by (specific date)
A runabout boat	A 16-ft. blue and white fiberglass boat with 50 h.p. outboard motor by (specific date)
A new car	A Buick Lesabre, 4 door, fully equipped by (specific date)

Write out your goals and place them where they can be seen—to constantly remind you. See yourself achieving these goals and keep them in your mind.

Our LONG RANGE GOALS should be three to five years in the future. The INTERMEDIATE GOALS should cover one year to three years. The SHORT RANGE GOALS should be on a daily, weekly and monthly basis, making sure your short range goals are broken down into realistic challenges that make a contribution to the intermediate goals and the intermediate goals make their contribution to the long range goals.

TURN INTENTIONS INTO COMMITMENTS

DEADLINES on all three goals are a must. DEADLINES make INTENTIONS become firm COMMITMENTS, keeping us from PROCRASTINATION. You know and I know of many people who have good intentions who never get started with their projects. When you make commitments with deadlines, it FORCES you into ACTION. DEADLINES also give you a CHECKING POINT to see if you are on SCHEDULE. Long range goals may overwhelm you unless you break them down into bite size pieces. THERE IS ONLY ONE WAY TO EAT AN ELEPHANT, AND THAT IS ONE BITE AT A TIME!

There is only one way to achieve your long range goals and that is by making your short range goals a reality—one bite at a time. Also, by setting your goals in this fashion you are automatically becoming GOAL-ORIENTED and not TASK-ORIENTED. You are becoming ACHIEVEMENT-ORIENTED and will not let the short term FRUSTRATIONS and DIS-APPOINTMENTS you have get the best of you.

If you keep your mind on your goals, you are less likely to become discouraged. Obstacles always show up when you take your eyes off the goal. I know many people who purposely do not write out their goals, and do not want to put deadlines on their goals. Why? I'll tell you why—When we turn INTENTIONS into firm COMMITMENTS we then have to get TOTALLY INVOLVED to bring that goal into reality. Too many people do not want to be committed or totally involved. I'm saying BE TOTALLY COMMITTED AND INVOLVED and then you will MAKE THINGS HAPPEN!

BIGGER GOALS = BIGGER PROBLEMS

"The hardest thing about milking cows," said the farmer, "is that they never stay milked."

That's true of a lot of things in life—you may even feel that way about your job or profession. No matter how much you get done, there's always an unfinished pile. No matter how many problems you take care of, more always seem to crop up.

But would we really want it any different? If people solved all the problems on their jobs and had no new ones to look forward to, what kind of jobs would they have left? And would anyone really be needed to fill them? Soft, comfortable, trouble-free jobs don't pay very well or last very long.

It's amazing how many people secretly look forward to the day when they'll be promoted to a better job with fewer problems. They forget that solving problems is what they are getting paid for. The higher the job, the tougher the problems.

It takes some people the better part of their careers to find this out. They envy the rewards and power of being a leader, but rarely appreciate the never-ending TROUBLES, FRUSTRATIONS, DIFFICULTIES and IRRITATIONS that go with it.

No one can advance very far in any line of work unless they are willing to come to grips with the problems associated with it. The bigger the job, the bigger the problems. PROBLEMS GIVE PEOPLE A CHANCE TO SUCCEED. If there were never any problems, how would we know how capable we are? REAL PROS welcome problems as a chance to show what they can do. They take, as personal challenges, every GOAL with a DEADLINE to be met, every difficult or unpleasant person they have to work with, every hard, demanding job they have to do.

You must expect problems, BUT if you have written out your goals, kept your eyes on the goals, have the A-K-A-W going for you in a positive way, you are totally committed and involved, you quickly learn that PROBLEM SOLVING is a very big part of ACHIEVING YOUR GOALS. The larger the goals you set—the larger the problems are going to be. YOU CAN TELL A MAN BY THE SIZE OF THE PROBLEMS THAT GET HIS GOAT!

You and I should thank God every night for the problems

we have. Problems become the stepping stones for greater goal achievement.

AIM HIGH

Make it a WORTHY, REALISTIC GOAL that you will be PROUD of when you achieve it. I know of too many people who do not HAVE GREAT EXPECTATIONS and they habitually sell themselves short either intentionally or unintentionally! Why? Because some people are just too lazy to spend the energy to achieve something worthwhile for themselves, their companies, and their families.

Recently, someone told me that he would lose his SELF-RE-SPECT if he wasn't getting a SENSE OF ACHIEVEMENT by WORKING HARD and INTELLIGENTLY toward his WORTHY GOALS. In order to be good at anything, we have to LIKE OURSELVES and have SELF-RESPECT. It doesn't hurt to PAT OURSELVES ON THE BACK when we have achieved WORTHY GOALS. Some people unintentionally aim too low and, thereby, never achieve a great amount in their careers because they have AIMED AT A LOW MARK. Perhaps this is what Professor William James, the father of modern psychology, meant when he said, "The average individual today is using and developing about 10% of his or her latent abilities, 90% of those treasures lie deep down inside of us unused. Comparing ourselves to the ocean, we are like the waves upon the sea compared to the oceans' mighty depths."

WORK OUT A DEFINITE PLAN OF ACTION

Many times goals fall short of achievement because effective, workable programs and plans for action to achieve such goals are not carefully thought out and formulated. CONCENTRATE and come up with concepts and principles of good planning to get from WHERE YOU ARE to WHERE YOU WANT TO BE. Be sure you FOLLOW UP and CONCENTRATE on the essentials.

None of us should ever feel that we have reached the top or peaked out. When we stand on the top rung of the ladder, there's only one way to go and that's down . . . Set even HIGHER GOALS, work out a DEFINITE PLAN OF ACTION, place DEADLINES on your goals and HAVE GREAT EXPECTATIONS. WE CAN DO ANYTHING WITH OUR LIVES AND ABILITIES THAT WE REALLY WANT TO DO. We must have a BURNING DESIRE TO SUCCEED and TRUE HEART POWER. What the mind of man can BELIEVE AND CONCEIVE, IT WILL ACHIEVE!

▲　　▲　　▲　　▲

"GARDLINES" *by Grant G. Gard*

DON'T TALK ABOUT THESE THINGS—DO THEM NOW!!

1. CREATE and VISUALIZE a bright future for yourself . . . YOU'LL STAY YOUNG.
2. CREATE and VISUALIZE the successful salesperson you want to be and get this PICTURE clearly in MIND. You are not what you are, but what you THINK YOU ARE!
3. CREATE and VISUALIZE worthy family goals, business goals, and improvement goals. Make them SPECIFIC, with DEADLINES.
4. CREATE and VISUALIZE your long term, intermediate, and short range goals and here be very SPECIFIC with DEADLINES.
5. AIM HIGH and HAVE GREAT EXPECTATIONS. Realize you are probably operating on about 10% of your latent abilities.
6. Pat yourself on the back and be PROUD OF YOURSELF when you make your WORTHY GOALS become a REALITY.

7. Be determined to have a BURNING DESIRE and a TRUE HEART POWER attitude in achieving your goals.
8. Zero in on YOUR TARGET.
9. Work out a DEFINITE plan and CONCENTRATE on essentials.
10. Focus on "RESULTS TO BE ACHIEVED" and not "TASK TO BE PERFORMED."
11. KEEP THINGS MOVING until your desired results are achieved!

▲   ▲   ▲   ▲

THOUGHT PROVOKING QUOTES

"Not failure, but low aim is crime."
—Lowell

"You must have long-range goals to keep you from being frustrated by short-range failures."
—Charles C. Noble

"No rule for success will work if you won't."
—Anonymous

"Great minds have purposes, others have wishes. Little minds are tamed and subdued by misfortunes; but great minds rise above them."
—Washington Irving

"Expect the best! It lies not in the past.
God ever keeps the good wine till the last.
Beyond the nobler work and sweeter rest,
    Expect the best!"
—William P. Merrill

"Life must be measured by thought and action, not by time."
—Sir John Lubbock

"What is faith unless it is to believe what you do not see?"
—St. Augustine

"In whatever position you find yourself determine first your objective."
—Marshal Ferdinand Foch

5 | *How to Find a Better Way*

The future belongs to the discontented.
Have you ever noticed how some people seem to come up with more than their share of good, practical ideas? Is it luck? Maybe, but I sure doubt that. Mostly, it's a matter of CARING, of STAYING NEW and of being keenly interested in seeing things done the best possible way.

People who are dissatisfied with the way things are currently being done are people most likely to make changes. THEIR DISCONTENTMENT MAKES THEM WANT TO DISCOVER NEW AND BETTER WAYS OF GETTING THINGS DONE.

GOOD IDEAS DON'T JUST HAPPEN. Usually they come to people who are bothered by problems. People who aren't aware of problems—who aren't bothered by them—wouldn't recognize good ideas for solving them.

Suppose, for example, that you are satisfied with the waste in your operation, be it waste in material, production or the waste of precious time. It all seems reasonable to you. What are the chances that you'll come up with an idea to better that situation? Very, very, small!

The key to getting good ideas is to be aware of problems and have a STAY NEW ATTITUDE—to want to improve in every respect. Look for the problems in your job—how could you improve your production, create an even better image for you and your company, how could your product be improved, your output increased, your costs reduced, and your sales increased?

Immerse yourself in a problem. Think about it day by day. Then, when you see the answer, you'll recognize it right away. It doesn't take a lot of brilliance to come up with good ideas. Just the RIGHT STAY NEW ATTITUDE, DESIRE, and PERSIS-TENCE.

Grow or Go. One sure way of staying out of trouble is to be open-minded and try to find NEW ideas to do an even better job—become NEW IDEA conscious. When we are GREEN, we are GROWING. When we are RIPE, we are ROTTING!! Always assume that you can do even better and that there is a better way of getting things done. I call this HAPPY DISCONTENT-MENT. STAY NEW!

I know of many businesses that are not existing now because they tried to continue old and dead practices and regardless of what business we are in we have to keep up with the latest skills and techniques if we are going to survive and thrive. A business either GROWS OR GOES.

In my little home town of Overton, Nebraska, there are now boards nailed up across the windows where glass used to be—busi-nesses no longer in existence because they didn't stay new. They tried to do business like it was done ten or twenty years ago and it just doesn't work.

BUILDINGS DON'T MAKE UP BUSINESSES—PEOPLE DO! We've got to stay competitive in this highly, fast changing, competitive world and realize that regardless of our occupation or business—We are in the PEOPLE BUSINESS. Solve peoples' problems and we stay in business.

WE EITHER GROW OR GO. These words are one of the reasons why there is such a high turnover rate in personnel. People are not willing to pay the price of success TO STAY NEW.

"I am doing alright" are the four worst words in the world. With this attitude you are NOT GROWING because you have fallen victim to routine and bad habits. You conform with the 95 percenters who have a NEGATIVE ATTITUDE and do not spend energy and effort to grow every day.

SEEK NEW IDEAS

Here's a simple THREE-STEP FORMULA to stay out of trouble.

Step 1. SEEK AND CREATE.

Seek and create new and better ideas to work with people and to sell yourself. Be looking for better ways to obtain desired results. Some of the things you can do is attend seminars, company meetings, talk to the boss, talk to other people in the company or outside of the company. Many times we pick up good ideas from outside people in the way they market their products and keep production high. Read good books on developing leadership and selling skills, listen to recorded messages—records and tapes. Mentally apply these new ideas to your situation. You will be surprised how many of these new ideas will work in your particular situation. You will be surprised how many of them will work when you get serious about improving your skills.

In addition to learning new ideas and techniques from others, you can also use your CREATIVE MIND to develop some new skills or products. Creativity is the most sought-after quality in leaders and salespeople today.

My friend, Gene Fleming in Hastings, Nebraska, was a tobacco salesman. In 1961, Gene was driving mile after mile between towns where he would make his calls. One day, Gene was making a usual drive and he saw cattle rubbing against barbed wire or home-made scratchers made from wire and gunny sack material soaked with a chemical oil. The purpose was so that the cattle would rub against these and automatically rub the chemical oil on their backs thus eliminating scabies, lice, bugs, etc.

Gene immediately saw a NEED and PROBLEM. He also used his imagination to CREATE and VISUALIZE a device that would be more efficient and thus help the farmers eliminate their problem. He designed automatic Rol-oil devices. The cattle would rub against them, turning them and getting a greater application of the chemical oil.

Gene is president of his own company and has gone nationwide with his idea. Needless to say, he went from a $300 to $400 a month tobacco salesman to a well-to-do executive.

You have CREATIVE ABILITY just as Gene Fleming had. Too many people accept things without really trying to improve them. Here are some ideas to help you use your CREATIVE ABILITY:

1. Check your ATTITUDE and be sure you are OPEN-MINDED to NEW IDEAS and SELL YOURSELF on the importance of doing things even better.
2. NEVER BE SATISFIED, you must assume everything can be improved.
3. Have CREATIVE THINK PERIODS and really use your imagination.
4. Have clearly in mind the PURPOSE of your creative session

by defining the thing you would like to work on or the problem.

5. Write down every idea you can think of and DO NOT EVALUATE THEM until you are through writing.

6. Have an INQUIRING MIND and never be concerned with what someone might say. (A lot of good ideas were ridiculed before being accepted).

7. Keep THINKING AND CONCENTRATING. Ask yourself, "How will it look better?" "Can the cost be cut?" "Could it be modified to have more potential?" "Is there a more time-saving way?" "Is there a phrase to use to help sell more?" "What do people really want or need?" "Could it save the company money?" "How can I bring more and better service to my prospects and clients?" "How can I keep the morale high and get the most production from my people?" You could go on and on. A lot of the ideas won't be usable but keep plugging and you'll be surprised what good ideas you can create. One good idea is all it takes to open up many new doors and avenues.

Creative Thinking is "future-oriented". It looks to the future and tries to find a more effective way to do things.

Judicial Thinking is "past-oriented". It relies on past experience in evaluating new ideas, methods and techniques.

The important thing is to keep both types of thinking in proper balance and not utilize one at the cost of neglecting the other. They compliment each other. Together they make an unbeatable combination.

Edison was asked: "It must be great to get inspired and then invent something." He replied, "No, I invent something and then I get inspired."

I have heard so many times: "MY SITUATION IS DIF-FERENT"—I don't buy that for the simple reason that the situation may be different, but the techniques used are very similar in producing desired results. I define successful managing and selling as "APPLYING OUR KNOWLEDGE WITH MOTIVATION SO THAT IT CAUSES PEOPLE TO REACT IN A POSITIVE WAY".

LACK OF KNOWLEDGE RETARDS
ACCOMPLISHMENT

I heard of a man who lived on the bank of the Mississippi River in a home that he and his wife had built. One day the man received a message that forced him to go into the city to complete a business transaction. He packed his suitcase, went down to the bank of the river and took the ferry across to the other side. He then got on the train which ran into the city.

When his business was completed, he found himself impatient to get home. He boarded the train knowing that he would not arrive home until after dark. When he arrived at the railroad station he could see the lights burning in the windows in his little home across the river. The ferry had quit running until morning. It was in the middle of winter and the river was partially frozen, so with the lights of his home to guide him, he began to inch his way across the river on the ice.

First he held a small tree to test whether or not the ice would hold his weight and he found that it would close to shore. He dropped to his knees and slowly began his long crawl home. After a considerable length of time he glanced back over his shoulder and by the dim light he could see that he was only a hundred feet from the shore he had just left.

It was about then that he felt weak but steady vibrations

on the ice. Soon he heard muffled hoof beats, they became louder and louder, and then he could see a team of horses pulling a sled across the ice toward him. He suddenly realized that the ice was strong enough to hold him, so he rose to his feet and ran the remaining distance to his house on the other side.

Lack of knowledge holds you back, RETARDS your ACCOMPLISHMENTS. It keeps you from doing the things you really want to do, but you can usually acquire the necessary knowledge and information quite easily if you will start looking for it.

Step 2. ACCEPT NEW IDEAS.

Minds are like concrete—thoroughly mixed and permanently set. *Our minds only let in what we want to hear . . .* the things with which we are in accord.

After you SEEK and CREATE new ideas, then the next mental process is to ACCEPT THE NEW IDEAS. Again I say . . . Don't be misled by the negatives—"Oh, those ideas are fine but they won't work for me". MAKE THEM WORK . . . CREATE and VISUALIZE how you can use them SUCCESSFULLY. Sure, not all ideas are going to be winners for you, but at least you are ACCEPTING NEW IDEAS and the ACCEPTANCE ATTITUDE is very important if you are going to meet and beat competition and create competition. Too many times we say: "I don't know anything about it, but I'm sure it won't work".

Step 3. PUT NEW IDEAS INTO ACTION.

After we SEEK, CREATE and ACCEPT, then the next thing that is a MUST is to get busy and put the NEW IDEAS into ACTION. Try them and use them in your OWN INDIVIDUAL WAY. Soap never got anything clean until it was applied!! Ideas never improved anything until they were applied!! DON'T BE AFRAID to try sound, practical ideas!! That's the way you GROW!!

I WANT TO KNOW IT ALL

Too many people have the "I KNOW IT ALL" attitude when they should have the "I *WANT* TO KNOW IT ALL" attitude. The head never swells until the mind stops growing. To "think" and to "learn" requires effort and some people just don't want to spend the effort. School is never out for the Pro!!

THERE IS ALWAYS ANOTHER LEVEL OF LEARNING

WHEN THE STUDENT IS READY, THE TEACHER IS THERE!! When we are ready for growth, there is always some way to find the answers . . . there is always a way to get to the next level of learning. For example, take a common old lead pencil . . . how is it made? One level of learning is to say it is made of wood, has lead in it and an eraser on the end of the pencil. THAT'S ONE LEVEL.

LET'S GO TO THE NEXT . . . The wood is a certain kind, a certain hardness, the lead is graphite and a certain hardness, the eraser is a certain synthetic and the eraser is attached to the wood with a metal band of a certain kind.

Now we know all about pencils! No, we don't! THERE'S ANOTHER LEVEL OF LEARNING. The material has certain molecular activities with protons and neutrons, etc., and we could go on and on to the next levels.

Let me ask you this: How do they put the lead in a pencil? Don't know? They halve the wood, lay the lead in and place the top half over the bottom half and glue it. What I am talking about is not how to get the lead in but HOW TO GET THE LEAD OUT!!

HOW SHARP IS YOUR AXE?

The foreman of a large lumber camp in the north woods was standing in front of his cabin one evening when he saw a young lad coming toward him on the trail leading to his cabin. He was a husky young fellow and he walked up and asked, "Are you the foreman?" The foreman said, "Yes, I am. What can I do for you?"

The young man replied, "I want a job". The foreman asked, "Have you ever cut trees?" The husky young man answered, "No, I never have, but I'm young, I'm strong and I'm eager to learn and am willing to work hard. I'll do a good job for you". So the foreman said, "All right, you go over to the bunkhouse and get a good night's sleep and at dawn I'll meet you right here and give you a job".

The next morning they met at dawn and they took a brand new axe with them. The foreman got the young man out in the forest and started him cutting trees. The first day the young fellow cut about two hundred trees. The next morning he started at the same time and quit at the same time and cut 165 trees. The third day he cut less than 100 trees. The foreman went out to see what was so wrong that his production was dropping off so rapidly.

The foreman said, "Young man, are you working as hard as you did the first day?" He replied that he was. "In fact," he said, "I'm even working harder and my third day I not only worked harder but I worked longer." The foreman asked, "Are you swinging the axe as fast?" The young man said, "Yes, even much faster". The foreman reached over and touched the blade of the axe and found it to be very dull. He said, "Young man, when did you last sharpen the blade of your axe?" The young man replied, "Foreman, I DIDN'T HAVE THE TIME TO STOP

AND SHARPEN MY AXE . . . I WAS TOO BUSY CHOPPING TREES''.

We do a similar thing with our lives. WE GET TOO BUSY TO TAKE THE TIME TO SHARPEN OUR AXE! We need to EXERCISE OUR THINKING before it becomes TOO NARROW, TOO DULL. We need to do something daily to keep our axe sharpened, to stay NEW in our PROFESSION. The person who keeps LEARNING stays YOUNG and NEW!! One of the greatest things in life is to keep our minds SHARP, YOUNG and NEW. Give a man a fish and you have fed him for today. Teach a man to fish and you have fed him for life!!

I am trying my best to teach and share with you some new ideas so that you will be fed for life by continuing the practice of these principles everyday.

PEOPLE RESIST CHANGE or "BUT WE'VE ALWAYS DONE IT THIS WAY" . . .

In working with high level management people, I can tell you one of their biggest challenges is getting people to accept and use new ideas. PEOPLE JUST SIMPLY RESIST CHANGE. They prefer to be left in their OWN COMFORT ZONE. The person who accepts and puts new ideas into effect is well on his way to the top because about 90 to 95% of the people resist change.

Bernard Baruch gave this formula for achievement: K + A = S . . . *Knowledge* plus *Action* equals *Success*. KEEP GETTING NEW KNOWLEDGE and PUT IT INTO ACTION NOW. Many times we think that putting new ideas into effect will slow us down . . . have you ever thought about how much PRODUCTION,

TIME, ENERGY, THOUGHT and MONEY it costs us NOT TO PUT NEW IDEAS INTO EFFECT?

A storekeeper fell behind in his payments to a supplier, and, furthermore, completely ignored three increasingly sharp letters demanding payment. Finally the supplier appeared in person, waving a hand full of unpaid bills in the storekeeper's face. The storekeeper thereupon astounded him by paying up in full without a moment's hesitation. "Why didn't you send me a check and save both of us all this unpleasantness?" demanded the supplier.

"I didn't have the cash to begin with," admitted the storekeeper, "so I copied your letters and mailed them out to the people who owed *me* money. The results were so gratifying I held up my payments to you till I could get your complete set of collection letters!!"

The storekeeper had a *positive mental attitude* about NEW IDEAS. He put the new ideas into ACTION and received gratifying rewards, just as you can do.

INSURE YOUR FUTURE

Just as insurance provides us with protection against being WIPED OUT by a storm, wind, hail, auto accident and major illness, a positive mental attitude about STAYING NEW insures our future against being left behind in this fast changing world. DON'T DELAY . . . START TODAY developing the right type of attitude about change and prepare yourself to cope with changes.

Leaders, salespeople, managers, parents . . . fall into one of three categories:

1. Those who, when placed in a changing situation, *can come up with the ideas* as to what needs to be done, can plan a procedure and can carry out that plan.

2. Those who, when placed in a changing situation, *if shown* what needs to be done, can plan a way to do it and carry out that plan.

3. Those who, when placed in a changing situation, *if shown* what needs to be done and *shown how* to do it, can then go ahead.

With the right type of attitude about staying new and FINDING A BETTER WAY, you can fall in the choice category of #1. This insures your FUTURE EARNING POWER. It is a great challenge, but it is a challenge that must be met if you are going to make your PLANS COME ALIVE and your GOALS A REALITY.

▲ ▲ ▲ ▲

"GARDLINES" *by Grant G. Gard*

DON'T TALK ABOUT THESE THINGS—DO THEM NOW!!

1. Have an OPEN MIND to NEW IDEAS.
2. Become NEW IDEA CONSCIOUS.
3. Be determined to GROW—not GO.
4. SEEK and LOOK for new ideas.
5. ACCEPT new ideas. Never say, "Why change? It's been done this way for the last 5 years".
6. Don't PROCRASTINATE about putting new ideas into ACTION.
7. RAISE your level of LEARNING about your profession. "When the student is ready . . . the teacher is there."
8. Do something daily to sharpen the axe . . . to stay NEW, SHARP and ALERT.
9. Don't fall victim to BAD HABITS, ROUTINE AND CONFORMITY.
10. THINK and CREATE for YOURSELF.
11. Have HAPPY DISCONTENTMENT.

▲　▲　▲　▲

THOUGHT PROVOKING QUOTES

"The world hates change, yet it is the only thing that has brought progress."

—Charles F. Kettering

"It is not the weathercock that changes, it is the wind."

—C. Desmoraline

"Consider how hard it is to change yourself and you'll understand what little chance you have trying to change others."

—Arnold Glasow

"Change is inevitable. The great question of our time is whether the change will be by consent or coercion."

—Bishop G. Bromley

"The only real equality is in the cementery."

—German Proverb

"A great many people think they are thinking when they are rearranging their prejudices and superstitions."

—Edward R. Murrow

"Most of us never recognize opportunity until it goes to work in our competitor's business."

—P. L. Andarr

"Lord, when we are wrong, make us willing to change. And when we are right, make us easy to live with."

—Peter Marshall

"Men do not stumble over mountains, but over molehills."

—Confucius

"What lies behind us and what lies before us are tiny matters compared to what lies within."

—Ralph Waldo Emerson

"The joy is in creating, not in maintaining."

—Vince Lombardi

6 | *Enthusiasm— The Little- Recognized Secret of Success*

PEOPLE ARE NOT PERSUADED BY WHAT WE SAY, ONLY BY WHAT THEY UNDERSTAND AND FEEL. Little Jimmy came home from school one afternoon and his mother asked him how his day had gone and what he had done in school. He sat down and for about 20 minutes told his mother all about the many things that he had done in school that day.

About a week later Jimmy's mother was busy ironing when Jimmy came home from school. She asked Jimmy to tell her all about his day at school. He uttered a couple of sentences and immediately went upstairs to change his clothes so that he could go out to play. On the way through the living room he passed by his busy mother and she said, "Jimmy, I don't understand this. Last week when I asked you all about your school activities, you spent at least 20 minutes telling me about them. BUT this afternoon when I asked you about school you spent about 20 or 30 seconds and now you are running out to play. I want to know why?"

Little Jimmy replied, "LAST WEEK, MOM, YOU *REALLY* WANTED TO KNOW, BUT TODAY IT REALLY DIDN'T MAKE ANY DIFFERENCE."

Jimmy felt exactly like his mother felt. We can't fool anybody. People around us are going to feel EXACTLY THE WAY WE FEEL.

Enthusiasm is the Key. A leader or salesperson has to transfer his or her KNOWLEDGE and FEELING in order to get desired, positive results. You can't give something to somebody else that you don't have yourself. ENTHUSIASM IS CONTAGIOUS . . . You have to have it before you can give it to anyone around you. ENTHUSIASM helps you to sell your ideas, concepts, products and yourself. People like to do business and work with a "LIVE WIRE" . . . a person who is EXCITED about the BENEFITS of the ideas and services and the things that can be done for others. STAY EXCITED . . . The Pro does!

MAKE THINGS HAPPEN

There are THREE TYPES OF PEOPLE . . .

Those who make it happen
Those who sit back and watch it happen
Those who wake up the next morning and say: "What did happen?"

Putting it another way there are those who are SELF STARTERS, those who you have to CRANK UP and those who you have to TOW IN.

Be determined to MAKE THINGS HAPPEN in your life. Don't sit back and watch the parade. At least be in it or better yet, LEAD IT! The lead mule is the only one that gets a change of scenery! You can't make a place for yourself under the sun if you keep sitting in the shade of the tree.

GET EXCITED ABOUT SOMETHING

I hear this many times . . . "I have nothing to get excited about" . . . Surely everyone can find many things each day to get EXCITED about . . . to turn themselves on. If you aren't excited about your profession, your services and your products, it is time to GET OUT.

One of the ways to TURN YOURSELF ON is to stop and think of the many BENEFITS and CONTRIBUTIONS you can offer your company, family and prospects . . . THAT should turn you on! If you or a member of your family are not listed in the local morning paper in the obituary column—that should be enough right there to get YOU TURNED ON and EXCITED! BE EXCITED THAT YOU ARE ALIVE TODAY and look for the GOOD instead of the BAD in each day. I know of many people in their 50's, 60's and 70's who are far more excited than some in their 20's and 30's. I know of many in their 20's and 30's who have already died and are just hanging on waiting to be buried.

ENTHUSIASM MAKES MIRACLES HAPPEN!!

I saw Aldon Hoppa, of Colorado Springs, really get TURNED ON in 1965. Aldon was a cabinet builder, doing a good job, but was not enthused about his job. He took advantage of a Leadership-Self Development Course and developed a very "EXCITED ATTITUDE" about himself, his new-found abilities and his future. He changed jobs . . . took a job with new challenges and has been really going great guns.

Al found that ENTHUSIASM is the LITTLE-RECOGNIZED SECRET of SUCCESS and ACHIEVEMENT. His excited attitude has motivated HIMSELF and OTHERS AROUND HIM. He is now the office manager of a large company in Denver. Needless to say, his income tripled in just six months after having changed jobs. He made his own breaks. Al didn't sit back and wait for things to happen, he made things happen. Al worked wisely . . . he found out that successful people must do things that failures won't do because successful people know those things MUST be done.

You can make things happen and increase your income just as Al did with increased excitement and enthusiasm.

ACT ENTHUSIASTIC AND
YOU WILL BE ENTHUSIASTIC

You can be animated and still not be enthused. Enthusiasm and excitement come from an inner attitude of true enjoyment or happiness. It's possible to be enthused without animation (sitting in church when the minister says something that turns you on or listening to a speech when the speaker talks about something that you can hardly wait to take out and put into practice). Usually, however, you become more animated when you become more enthused.

William James pointed out that, "Action and feeling go together; and, by regulating the action which is under the most direct control of the will, we can indirectly regulate the feeling which is not." So to feel enthusiastic . . . *ACT* ENTHUSIASTIC AND YOU'LL *BE* ENTHUSIASTIC.

Please don't confuse enthusiasm with noise. Webster says that Enthusiasm is "Ardent zeal, or interest, fervor." Fervor is "Intensity of expression." Webster doesn't say a word about noise, yelling or stamping. Real enthusiasm always comes from the inside out. It is an internal condition—a joyous excitement.

WHICH CATEGORY ARE YOU IN?

I compare people with three different types of glasses . . . all being filled with water. In the first glass, I drop an aspirin—nothing happens, but that's the way with lots of people and that's how they radiate.

In the second glass, I drop in some Bromo Seltzer—it bubbles up fast and dies down quickly. That's the way with some people. They may start the day good but little things come along that cause discouragement and down they go. That type the boss has to talk to frequently to keep him fired up, but it's just like the Bromo Seltzer, it doesn't last long . . . the fire is all gone.

Then there is the long-acting type and that's the Alka Seltzer type . . . that person is always excited, always sparkling. That's the person who is always making things happen, handling problems by going through them rather than running around them, seeing things in a positive successful way.

I hope everyone of you will take an oath right now to have the "Alka Seltzer" type of enthusiasm the rest of your lives. EXCITED PEOPLE GET THINGS DONE!!

TURN MINUSES INTO PLUSES

PEP TALKS . . . use them every day, several times a day. I give myself 20 to 30 pep talks a day. I *know* they help to turn MINUSES into PLUSES. Pep talks help you to see things in a POSITIVE WAY rather than in a NEGATIVE WAY.

PEP TALKS should be SHORT, POSITIVE and should TELL YOURSELF what you are going to do SUCCESSFULLY. You should use your IMAGINATION and, here again, CREATE and VISUALIZE yourself doing the thing successfully that you are about to undertake.

Many people tell me that they give themselves PEP TALKS when they get up in the morning, before each undertaking throughout the day and before retiring in the evening. Coaches and pro ball players use many PEP TALKS each day with the ball club members. If it will work for them, it will work for you. I know!! I use them and they sure help me. PEP TALKS INCREASE PRODUCTION, EFFECTIVENESS AND SALES!!

WHAT'S AROUND YOU IS YOU

You can tell what people are thinking by what's around them. If they have good clientele, employees and managers around them and have been successful, then you know they have been enthused. They have been SENDING OUT THE RIGHT KINDS OF "SIGNALS" from their minds. If they have nothing around them in the way of friends, associates and clientele, you know they have been transmitting nothing . . . they get nothing back. It's all up to you as a leader or salesperson to determine what's going to be around you. PEOPLE ARE KNOWN BY THE COMPANY THEY KEEP.

ELIMINATE THE NEGATIVE—ACCENTUATE THE POSITIVE

You can use all the ideas in this book to help you get the things you want from life. I know you aren't used to giving yourself "POSITIVE PEP TALKS" and you may not be fully excited about life.

The only thing holding you back is you—old habits, old attitudes and your "COMFORT ZONE". I know—I was negative, comfortable in my own little world of negative thinking and busy thinking of reasons why I couldn't do things I wanted to do. Excuses!! Don't waste any more time thinking about and visualizing old negative pictures.

ELIMINATE THE NEGATIVE—start a whole new exciting chapter in your life by, RIGHT NOW, NOT TOMORROW, ACCENTUATING THE POSITIVE. Use your IMAGINATION to create the NEW YOU. Establish POSITIVE, SUCCESSFUL PICTURES in your mind as to exactly the type of person you want to be. Establish a new, higher, greater comfort zone. Establish what you really want around you in the way of clients, friends and the tangibles of life and see yourself having these things from life.

A man from Okmulgee, Oklahoma, in his early 30's, came to me and complained that business was bad and that he just wasn't making it. Nice looking fellow, friendly, but very negative. I suggested that he consider changing from his negative thought pattern. He had mental B.O. bad! Every time he opened his mouth it was negatively! I wish I could put a happy ending to his story, but the last I heard of him he had failed again and was looking for something else to do.

He found it too difficult to break the old habits and couldn't see himself succeeding in life. It's not easy—I used to smoke and it was hard to quit, but I had the determination to succeed and I did. That's the key here—Have the DETERMINATION to really want to ELIMINATE THE NEGATIVE and ACCENTU-ATE THE POSITIVE. The rewards are there if you just DO IT and DO IT NOW!

LOOK—ACT—FEEL ENTHUSIASTIC

Ron C., who in his 30's quit the ministry, never had sold a thing and went into the life insurance business. The manpower turn-over is high in that field. Yet this man made the One Million Dollar Round Table his first year because he was determined to do the "Right Things Right" and that's what we are talking about in this book . . . Look—Act—Feel Enthusiastic.

I have watched Ron work. It's a pleasure to see a man have such a deep DESIRE, be so DETERMINED and be so DEDICAT-ED. I have seen Ron drive 200 miles at night, after working a full day, to sit in on a session where he could pick up new ideas to help him sell. I have seen him drive in snowstorms to keep appointments—many people would have called the prospect and cancelled. He is eager to do the job right. His success just didn't happen . . . he made it happen! He's a good salesman, a good office manager. He attracts the right kinds of people around him. He leads by setting a first-rate example.

Look—Act—Feel Enthusiastic. Have the DESIRE, DETER-MINATION and DEDICATION to build the right things around you and enjoy the success that Ron is enjoying!

I am going to share with you what I think is one of the most significant statements I have ever heard . . . "OUR SUC-CESS IS DEPENDENT UPON THE TYPES OF PEOPLE WE CAN ATTRACT AND INFLUENCE." Reread that . . . it's great. Enthusiasm and excitement, positive PEP TALKS . . . put you in the right frame of mind to ATTRACT and INFLUENCE people. Lose your ENTHUSIASM for your job, for your family, your profession and for living and you are through. EXCITED PEOPLE MAKE THINGS HAPPEN!!

BALANCE LOGIC AND EMOTION

Your job as a successful leader or salesperson is to use enough LOGIC to educate people and yet make people FEEL EMOTION-ALLY as you do about your product, ideas, concepts or service.

Using ENTHUSIASM helps to let people know how YOU FEEL about your ideas, services and products and will get them excited also. Remember you have to TRANSMIT it before it can be received by other people. Transmit the RIGHT SIGNAL OUT and you'll get the RIGHT "FEED BACK" back from everyone around you.

If you lead and sell with all logic and no emotion, you usually leave your clients, associates and employees very well-educated, but not emotionally involved.

If you use all emotion and not enough logic to satisfy their minds, you will not get full production, cooperation and desired results.

Use a balance of logic and emotion so that their minds and hearts are BOTH saying "Yes" and then you will be known as a real "People Builder."

SUCCESSFUL EXPERIENCES BUILD SELF-CONFIDENCE

I have noticed also that enthusiasm helps to build self-confidence. Why? Because when you are excited you are positive and get positive results. Nothing builds self-confidence like doing things successfully. One success upon another builds confidence in people. You can read all the books on self-confidence, but it still takes SUCCESSFUL EXPERIENCES to build self-confidence.

You can study all types of books on flying and listen to the instructor, but until you fly the plane by yourself and put into practice what you have learned, YOU ARE NEVER REALLY CONFIDENT. Every successful experience builds confidence. We all fear the unknown and become nervous. I have noticed that enthusiasm helps people to overcome their fears, their excessive nervousness and their timidity.

SOME NERVOUSNESS IS GOOD! It keys you up so you want to do an even better job. You have to learn to control your nervousness . . . get enthused about your opportunities, ideas and service and you'll be surprised how excessive nervous tension leaves.

Look at it this way . . . No one has ever paid to see old work horses run a race. People love to see and will bet on spirited horses, nervous, champin' at the bit horses, because they know it takes that quality to win. People love to see horses that are so excited that they can hardly wait to get started.

One day out at the race track, my youngest son, Alan, said, "Dad, you ought to bet on #6. He's so fired up they can hardly get the jockey on his back." Sure enough, he came in first!

It's good for people to GET FIRED UP! They are the ones who come in "first place" and win the blue ribbons.

DO THE THING YOU FEAR TO DO AND FEAR WILL LEAVE. The positive approach cuts down fear. *I won't say it will take away all of the butterflies, but it will sure help to get them flying in formation.* Courage is not the absence of FEAR; it is the mastery of it!

EVERYONE HAS FEAR AND NERVOUSNESS

Don't think that you are abnormal if you have some fear and nervousness . . . everyone does. Some fear and nervousness is good. It gets us keyed up, gets the adrenalin flowing and gets us ready for action. The Key . . . Learn to CONTROL IT and DRIVE ON in spite of it and MAKE IT WORK FOR YOU. You'll quickly have that "hold back" feeling licked by USING THE ENTHUSIASTIC APPROACH.

"GARDLINES" *by Grant G. Gard*

DON'T TALK ABOUT THESE THINGS—DO THEM NOW!!

1. Be determined to MAKE THINGS HAPPEN for you, for your company and for your family.
2. Don't sit back and watch things happen . . . "DON'T WATCH THE PARADE GO BY, LEAD IT."
3. Be EXCITED that you are alive today. Have the "Excited Attitude".
4. Use 10 to 20 positive PEP TALKS daily.
5. Analyze "What's around me"—friends and clientele.
6. ATTRACT and INFLUENCE the right type of people for your success.
7. Overcome fear and excessive nervousness by taking a much more ENTHUSIASTIC approach to your selling.
8. Have a strong desire not to let FEAR defeat you.
9. Make yourself a SELF-CONFIDENT PERSON by making successful things happen on a daily basis. Others will have confidence in you in direct proportion to the amount of self-confidence you have in yourself.
10. ELIMINATE the NEGATIVE—ACCENTUATE the POSITIVE.

▲　▲　▲　▲

THOUGHT PROVOKING QUOTES

"Enthusiasm is self-confidence in action."
—Franklin Field

"They conquer who believe they can. He has not learned the lesson of life who does not each day surmount a fear."
—Ralph Waldo Emerson

"You become enthusiastic by acting enthusiastic. Act enthusiastic and you'll be enthusiastic."
—Frank Bettger

7 | *Avoiding the Hazards of Conformity*

Know What Is Right and Do It. As a boy growing up, I used to look up to my father with a great amount of respect and admiration. He was a great leader and he taught me many very valuable lessons. One of the greatest lessons he taught me was the tremendous importance of DECIDING WHAT IS RIGHT, TAKING ACTION ON IT, AND REFUSING TO LISTEN TO THE "AGINERS"!

Dad was an excellent baseball umpire and just about every Sunday afternoon I would go with him and mother to watch the baseball game. Many times I used to dislike what I was seeing and hearing . . . you see, Dad was the home plate umpire and the instant he would *make a close call* you would hear and see the aginers, the GRANDSTAND UMPS, you could hear them "booing" and you could see them "throwing pop and beer bottles."

One day I asked Dad why he continued "umping" when he received absolutely no pay and in many games he would have to take that excessive heckling. His reply was a classic, "First of all I *love* the game. Secondly, those players *need* me badly." Then he went on to say, "I make the *best call* I possibly can, a call that I feel is honest and right. I know all of my decisions will not always please the whole crowd. What kind of an umpire would I be if I was just there to please the crowd?"

My dad was doing exactly the things we MUST DO TO REALLY BE A "PRO". He was doing what he loved to do, he was doing it very well, he was fulfilling a real need and he was not afraid to make decisions . . . even though he knew the MASSES would sometimes BOO him and be AGAINST him. HE CONTROLLED THE GAME. THE CROWD, WHO WAS WATCHING THE ACTION, DIDN'T CONTROL HIM.

BELIEVE THE NEGATIVES AND YOU ARE THROUGH

One of my greatest challenges in dealing with people was "How do I COPE with all of the NEGATIVE-THINKING PEO-PLE that I come in contact with?" I would hear every kind of person talking in negative terms about: His company; the people who live in the area; the products; it just can't be done here; people here are different; no money in the area; the economy is tight, etc. . . . . I could go on and on.

FARMERS, BUSINESSPEOPLE, DOCTORS, ATTOR-NEYS, EXECUTIVES and SALESPEOPLE that I thought were positive thinkers, I found out real quick-like, have MENTAL HALITOSIS, STINKIN' THINKIN', just like anyone else. I'm amazed how some men and women have become as successful as they have when you really get to know them and hear them talk.

I went into the little town of Holdrege, Nebraska, to develop a Self-Improvement Leadership and Communications seminar in the fall of 1960. It was around Thanksgiving and three service clubs turned down my sponsorship. I couldn't get one positive signal from anyone. So I decided to organize the program on a "one to one basis". Professional people and community leaders turned me down—it was the wrong time of the year with Christmas coming and it was their annual "Harvest of Sales". Farmers turned me down—the pig crop didn't turn out as good as they expected; cattle had shipping fever; corn was still in the fields; wheat crop not good. Gee, I really had built up a real case *against* putting on a seminar in that community. Two other men had tried and failed in this country town.

I knew I would talk to my boss on the week-end, so I really needed as many "FAILURE EXCUSES" as I could get to BUILD a STRONG CASE FOR MYSELF as to all the reasons why there could NOT be a seminar in that farming community.

The boss called and I gave him all the EXCUSES . . . he listened and then said this to me (which was the turning point in my career) . . . he said, "OK, I just want you to know that they put on a full seminar of 40 in McCook and a full seminar in Grand Island . . . each town about 70 miles away . . . they have the same businesspeople, the same pigs, the same cattle, the same wheat, the same corn, etc. and the same time of the year."

He didn't say another word, he didn't have to. I CHANGED MY ATTITUDE and two weeks later, the second week in December, had a full seminar of 40 lined up. I began to talk about the BENEFITS and END RESULTS of the seminar and all the REASONS THEY SHOULD DO IT *NOW,* not after January 1st, and my new THINKING WAS CONTAGIOUS, IT WORKED. I made new, positive mind pictures of me doing this successfully. The mind pictures became a reality . . . as they always do!

The same people who were turning me down were now my supporters. This experience taught me *well* the tremendous IMPORTANCE OF WHAT WE THINK, WHAT WE IMAGINE, and WHAT WE CREATE IN OUR MINDS CAN BECOME A REAL-

ITY. It taught me *very well* to " BE WARY OF WHO INFLU-ENCES WHOM". I was conforming to the many negatives. They were controlling me and destroying my ability to GET THINGS DONE SUCCESSFULLY.

STAY IN CONTROL

There is always the negative element trying to wreck things for the POSITIVE THINKER AND POSITIVE BUILDER, but we, as positive thinkers and builders, have to be strong enough not to let the NEGATIVES INFLUENCE US IN THE SLIGHT-EST. We have to be strong enough to stand on our own CONVIC-TIONS, BELIEFS AND IDEAS AND DO WHAT WE THINK AND KNOW IS RIGHT FOR US.

ARE YOU A WRECKER OR A BUILDER

I watched them tearing a building down,
    A gang of men in a busy town.
With a ho-heave-ho and a lusty yell
    They swung a beam and the sidewall fell.
I asked the foreman, "Are those men skilled,
    And the men you'd hire if you had to build?"
He gave a laugh, said "No, indeed;
    Just common labor is all I need.
I can easily wreck in a day or two
    What builders have taken a year to do."
I thought to myself as I went my way,
    "Which of these roles have I tried to play?
Am I a builder who works with care,
    Measuring life by the rule and square?
Am I shaping my deeds to a well-made plan,
    Patiently doing the best I can?
Or am I a wrecker, who walks the town
    Content with the labor of tearing down?"

—Author Unknown

Are you a WRECKER or a BUILDER? Sure, we should listen to the advice of others provided that they have achieved something worthwhile with their lives and we can respect them, but remember ADVICE from the NEGATIVES and WRECKERS is CHEAP, you can "BUY" it all day long.

DO YOUR OWN THINKING

I had many people try to discourage me from going into the speaking profession and self-improvement field—"It's overcrowded"; "You'll never make it"; "It's not for you". But it was only a short time later that I heard remarks like: "Gosh, I knew all the time that you could do it." "I knew you were going to make it." RESPECT others, but DON'T BELIEVE THEM because there's only one person in the world LIKE YOU and that IS YOU.

BE GLAD YOU ARE YOU, listen to the Pros and the people you respect for their accomplishments but STAND ON YOUR OWN CONVICTIONS and be a DETERMINED AND DEDICATED person to yourself, your family, your product and your company. DO YOUR OWN THINKING, don't follow the guy down the street . . . he may not know where he is going!! Ninety-five percent of the people have no worthy goals set for themselves.

DON'T IMITATE OTHERS

I have noticed that people who have their GOALS written out and know where they are going are usually not persuaded by the negatives. They are strong enough to stand on their OWN BELIEFS and CONVICTIONS. I have also noticed those who have their goals written out and know where they are going DO NOT TRY TO IMITATE OTHERS. They are individuals and know that it is suicide to imitate other people as we all have our own personalities and abilities. We have to develop them in our own INDIVIDUAL STYLE.

IF WE CAN'T BE SUCCESSFUL BEING OURSELVES, WE'LL SURE LOUSE IT UP TRYING TO BE SOMEONE ELSE.

I was interviewing the president of a bank in Nebraska several years ago and I'll never forget what he told me when I asked him how he got to be bank president.

He said, "I was working as a teller and trying to imitate the executives. One day I said to myself, 'That's all wrong, I have to be myself.' I forgot about everyone's qualities and started developing my own in my own individual way. I soon received a promotion because I was better than I thought I was."

Brulloff, the great Russian painter, once corrected a pupil's painting. The pupil looked in amazement at the altered drawing and exclaimed: "Why, you have touched it only a tiny bit, but it is quite another thing." Brulloff replied, "Art begins where the tiny bit begins." That is as true in a profession as it is in art . . . that "tiny bit of you" makes the difference!

There is no other human being in the world like you. Hundreds of millions of people have two eyes and a nose and a mouth, but none of them looks precisely like you . . . none of them has exactly your traits, personality, methods and mind. Few people will talk and express themselves like you do. YOU HAVE AN INDIVIDUALITY. It is your most precious possession. Cherish it and DEVELOP IT TO THE FULLEST. *It is your only claim to importance.* There's GENIUS in all of us if we'll look for it and BELIEVE IN OURSELVES enough.

I KNOW I CAN

If you think you are beaten, you are.

If you think you dare not, you don't.

If you'd like to win, but you think you can't, it's almost a cinch you won't.

If you think you'll lose, you've lost.

If you are afraid to fly, you'll spill.

For out in the world you find success begins with a will.

Many a race is lost, 'ere even a step is run and many a coward fails, 'ere even his work's begun.

Think big and your deeds will grow.

Think small and you'll fall behind.

Think that you can and you will.

It's all in the state of mind.

If you think you are outclassed, you are.

You've got to think high to rise.

You've got to be sure of yourself, before you can win a prize.

Life's battle doesn't always go to the stronger or faster man.

But sooner or later the man who wins is the fellow who thinks he can.

—Anonymous

BE IN THE TOP 5%

STAND OUT IN YOUR WORK!! Here again the negatives will attack you, but remember it's better to stand out in the top 5% than to get lost in the bottom 95%. Be known as a real DOER rather than an AGINER. Remember, PEOPLE DON'T TAKE A SHOT AT YOU IF YOU HAVEN'T GOT YOUR HEAD ABOVE THE WATER!! THE HIGHER YOU GO . . . THE LONELIER IT GETS . . . because fewer people have been able to accomplish with their lives what you have accomplished with yours. But also remember that the HIGHER UP YOU GO, THE

LESS COMPETITION YOU HAVE. Not too many people have the real burning desire (wishes, yes), the heart power to do what you are doing. We not only have to MEET COMPETITION, but we also have to CREATE COMPETITION!!

Give your family, your church, your profession, the world the very best that you have. The best will come back to you as described by Madeline S. Bridges when she wrote:

LIFE'S MIRROR

There are loyal hearts, there are spirits brave,
There are souls that are pure and true;
Then give to the world the best you have,
And the best will come back to you.

Give love, and love to your life will flow,
A strength in your utmost need;
Have faith, and a score of hearts will show
Their faith in your work and deed.

Give truth, and your gift will be paid in kind,
And honor will honor meet;
And the smile which is sweet will surely find
A smile that is just as sweet.

Give sorrow and pity to those who mourn;
You will gather in flowers again.
The scattered seeds from your thought outborne
Though the sowing seemed but vain.

For life is the mirror of king and slave,
'Tis just what we are and do;
Then give to the world the best you have
And the best will come back to you.

"GARDLINES" *by Grant G. Gard*

DON'T TALK ABOUT THESE THINGS—DO THEM NOW!!

1. Listen to others, then ask yourself, "AM I LETTING OTHER PEOPLE RUN MY LIFE—PERHAPS MY BUSINESS OR MY HOME?"
2. Seek the advice of only TOP NOTCH PEOPLE when you need consultation.
3. " BE WARY OF WHO INFLUENCES WHOM."
4. Be a truly DEDICATED and DETERMINED person—dedicated and determined to give your best to your profession, your product and your family.
5. Be a REAL DOER; a REAL BUILDER.
6. Be determined to develop a REAL BURNING DESIRE, THE HEART POWER to achieve your goals without letting the negatives influence you.
7. Be determined not only to MEET COMPETITION, but also to CREATE COMPETITION.
8. Never think you are beaten or outclassed. RISE TO EVERY OCCASION.
9. Don't be guilty of being a "wrecker."
10. Don't let the negatives of life DESTROY what you have.

▲   ▲   ▲   ▲

THOUGHT PROVOKING QUOTES

"The way to do things is to begin."
    —Horace Greeley

"There's nothing bad or good but thinking makes it so."
    —Shakespeare

"To accept good advice is but to increase one's own ability."
    —Goethe

"The important thing in life is to have a great aim and to possess the aptitude and the perserverance to attain it."

—Goethe

"As he thinketh in his heart, so is he . . . If God be for us, who can be against us?"

—Old Testament

"Every time a man puts a new idea across, he finds ten men who thought of it before he did—but they only thought of it."

—Henry G. Weaver

"To look is one thing. To see what you look at is another. To understand what you see is a third. To learn from what you understand is still something else. But to act on what you learn is all that really matters, isn't it?"

—Charles F. Kettering

"Oversleeping is a mighty poor way to make your dreams come true."

—Unknown

"No one gets very far unless he accomplishes the impossible at least once a day."

—Elbert Hubbard

"To feel brave, act as if we were brave, use all of our will to that end; and a courage fit will very likely replace the fit of fear."

—William James

"I have found that if I have faith in myself and in the idea I am tinkering with, I usually win out."

—Charles F. Kettering

"One ought never to turn one's back on a threatened danger and try to run away from it. If you do that, you will double the danger. But if you meet it promptly and without flinching, you will reduce the danger by half. Never run away from anything. Never!!"

—Winston Churchill

Take time for work; it is the price of success.
Take time to think; it is the source of power.
Take time to play; it is the secret of youth.
Take time to read; it is the foundation of wisdom.
Take time to be friendly; it is the road of happiness.
Take time to dream; it's hitching your wagon to a star.
Take time to love; it is the highest joy of life.
Take time to laugh; it is the music of the soul.

—Anonymous

"Enthusiasm is the vital element toward the individual success of every man or woman."

—Conrad Hilton

"Inferior complexes are seldom more than senseless timidities that rob us of courage, sap ambition and sap enterprise."

—Henry Link

"Don't attempt to lose your nervousness!! Use it!! Make it work for you!!"

—Frank Bettger

"Nervousness is the price you pay for being a race horse instead of a work horse."

—Professor Ormand Drake

"Nervousness is persuasive; artifice, just the reverse."

—Aristotle

8 | *Happiness Is Taking Possession of Today*

Happiness is Within. HAPPINESS is CREATED from WITHIN. I have found that external conditions have very little to do with a person's HAPPINESS . . . IT'S ALL IN HOW WE THINK!!

Two men looked out of prison bars, one saw mud and the other saw stars.

What will make one person happy will make another person sad. We are just about as happy as we want to be. HAPPINESS is a REFLECTION of our ATTITUDE about PEOPLE and THINGS. I don't know what would make you happy, but I can sure tell you this . . . People like to be around happy people, not ones who go around with scowls on their faces!

Remember, an IMPRESSION IS MADE WITHIN 20 to 30 SECONDS after you are face to face with another person. HAPPINESS IS TODAY . . . NOT OFF IN THE DISTANT FUTURE. Start the day Happy!! Think yourself Happy!!

So you say, "I don't feel like smiling—I don't feel happy"—Do this—act as if you are already happy and soon you will have the feeling of being that happy, jolly person.

Dr. George W. Crane said, "Act the way you'd like to be and soon you'll be the way you act." And Professor William James of Harvard said, "The sovereign voluntary path to cheerfulness, if our cheerfulness be lost, is to sit up cheerfully and to act and speak as if cheerfulness were already there."

Everyone wants to be happy and, as far as I know, there is only one way to achieve happiness . . . THINK HAPPINESS— ACT HAPPY. You can control your thoughts and you can become any type of person you want to become. You can create your own circumstances and conditions.

LOVE WHAT YOU DO

One evening when Thomas Edison came home from work, his wife said to him, "You've worked long enough without a rest. You must take a vacation."

"But where on earth would I go?" asked Edison.

"Just decide where you would be the happiest and go there," suggested his wife.

Edison hesitated. "Very well," he said finally. "I'll go tomorrow."

THE NEXT MORNING HE WAS BACK AT WORK IN HIS LABORATORY!

Yes . . . LOVE YOUR WORK! You do well what you love to do and you love to do what you do well. Seldom have I ever seen a highly successful and happy person who didn't love what he or she was doing!

IS YOUR BASKET EMPTY?

Many years ago, an Indian princess was called to the tepee of her father, the Chief. She put on her finest dress, combed her hair and made her way to the tepee. The Chief looked at her and said, "My daughter, today is your birthday, today you have become a woman. Your first duty as a woman of the tribe will be to go out and select the finest field of corn, then select the finest row in that field and then go down the row selecting only the finest ears of corn and fill your basket. Remember, daughter, that once you have passed an ear of corn you may not go back again."

So the princess made her way to the corn fields where she selected the finest field of corn . . . picking the best row she could. Then she started down that row feeling the ears as she went. She felt one ear that was too hard, the next ear too soft, the next irregular, the next too small and so on down the row. To her amazement she soon found herself at the END OF THE ROW AND HER BASKET WAS STILL EMPTY.

Many of us go through life ignoring the GREAT OPPORTU-NITIES OF TODAY, we find THINGS WRONG with living this very minute, this very day. We spend most of our time waiting for something good to happen in the future, PUTTING OFF LIVING TODAY, PUTTING OFF HAPPINESS. It's so easy to forget that this is life. LIFE IS WHAT HAPPENS TO YOU WHILE YOU ARE MAKING OTHER PLANS!!

We have a tendency to look for the "bad" and "wrong" in people and things. We are only hurting ourselves when we do this. Make it a habit right now to look for the good in everyone and everything. Let's create happiness for others without expecting anything in return. Yes, we'll be much happier, but don't just do and say nice things for a selfish reason.

Make happiness for others just for the inner joy it can bring them. Our happiness will take care of itself. If we look for the good and create happiness for others as well as ourselves, we'll never reach the end of a day, week or life with an "EMPTY BASKET".

LETTING BEETLES GET YOU DOWN?

On the slope of Long's Peak in Colorado lies the ruin of a huge tree. Naturalists say that it stood for some four hundred years. It was a seedling when Columbus landed at San Salvadore. It was half grown when the Pilgrims settled at Plymouth. During the course of its long life, it was struck by lightning fourteen times.

It, no doubt, had weathered literally thousands of storms. It survived them all. At the end, however, an army of beetles attacked the tree and they leveled it to the ground. These small insects, hardly larger than a finger nail, ate their way through the bark and gradually destroyed the very heart of the tree by their tiny but incessant attacks. This tremendous forest giant—this giant that age had not withered, that lightning had not blasted, that storms had not subdued, fell at last before beetles so small that a man could crush them between his forefinger and thumb.

Life is something like that battling giant of the forest. Rare storms and lightning blasts of life are somehow survived. It's the beetles of worry, stress, fear, tension that destroy happiness and success if they are allowed to exist. FEAR, WORRY, STRESS, and TENSION DESTROY HAPPINESS.

DON'T LET PROBLEMS GET YOUR GOAT

When you are complaining about so many things, ask yourself: "What would happen if all of the things I am worrying about and complaining about would be completely taken away from me?" If they would be completely taken away from you, I'll bet you would want them back in a hurry! Try using this phrase when things go sour: "THINGS COULD ALWAYS BE WORSE and be THANKFUL that you have the many GOOD THINGS that you do have and also be THANKFUL that you have the CHALLENGES each day that you have."

Challenges make us GROW if we take the RIGHT ATTITUDE about them and solve them as we live each day, one day at a time and one challenge at a time.

Don't put off solving challenges! A challenge is a challenge until you take the action to produce the results that you want. A lot of people run and hide from challenges or problems. They feel if they just don't think about them, they'll go away. Not so and you know it! Take action as soon as possible, then your mind will clear.

As you solve the challenges of the day, be thankful that you did so and be thankful for the opportunity to grow. We learn from our successes and challenges and failures. When solving challenges, keep your EMOTIONS under control. EVERY ADVERSITY IS AN OPPORTUNITY TO BECOME AN EVEN BETTER PERSON. It's all in how we, as individuals, look at things. A MAN IS NO BIGGER THAN THE THINGS THAT GET HIS GOAT. Be big in your thinking and resolve to be that happy, well-balanced, mature person you really want to be.

DON'T WEAR YOUR WORRIES ON YOUR SLEEVE

Leave your worries out of your work or your production will go down fast. On the other hand, leave your job at the office when you go home in the evening or your home life will deteriorate. PEOPLE DON'T WANT TO HEAR ABOUT YOUR PROBLEMS.

Eighty percent of the people don't care about your problems and the other 20% are actually glad that you have problems, just to find someone more miserable than they are. One of the worst things about worry is that it destroys our ability to think.

WORRY IS LIKE A ROCKING CHAIR—IT WILL GIVE US SOMETHING TO DO BUT WON'T GET US ANYWHERE. If you really want to test your memory, just try to think of the things that were worrying you last week at this time.

It is not the work, but the worry,
    That drives all sleep away,
As we toss and turn and wonder
    About the cares of the day.
Do we think of the hands' hard labour,
    Or the steps of the tired feet?
Ah, no! but we plan and wonder
    How to make both ends meet.

It is not the work, but the worry,
    That makes us troubled and sad.
That makes us narrow and sordid
    When we should be cheery and glad.
There's a shadow before the sunlight,
    And ever a cloud in the blue,
The scent of the rose is tainted,
    The notes of the song are untrue.

It is not the work, but the worry,
    That makes the world grow old,
That numbers the years of its children
    Ere half their story is told;
That weakens their faith in heaven
    And the wisdom of God's great plan.
Ah! 'tis not the work, but the worry
    That breaks the heart of man.
                    —*Anonymous*

It is not hard work that tears people down. It is usually worry that "wrecks" people. It's not physical fatigue that keeps people from sleeping, it's usually mental fatigue, stress, emotional disturbances and the petty worries of life that make people toss and turn in bed and pace the floor.

The story is told of the husband, Joe, who was a worrier from the word go. One night about 3 A.M., his wife heard Joe downstairs pacing back and forth across the carpet. She went downstairs and said, "Joe, what in the world are you worrying about tonight?" He said, "Hon, I'm worrying about that $200 that I owe John next door."

She said, "I'll fix that." She went to the window, pushed it open and shouted, "John, you know that $200 Joe owes you? Well, you ain't going to get it." Then she turned to Joe and said, "Get upstairs and get back to bed. Let's let John worry about it for awhile."

I am not saying don't pay your bills, but I *am* saying that we take ourselves too seriously and burden ourselves with too many job and family worries . . . many times to the point that we lose our effectiveness on the job and at home.

One of the best cures for WORRY is LAUGHTER. I know when I'm laughing I have a hard time thinking of the negatives. When I'm HAPPY and LAUGHING I'm positive and my mind is full of GOOD THOUGHT PICTURES.

Laughter is God's hand upon a troubled world. Few comics have made the world laugh as much as Zasu Pitts. She was one of the first women to turn comedy into a major medium, the movies. To millions of people fortunate enough to have seen her in the films of the THIRTIES, her name remains synonymous with comedy.

The world might never have heard of Zasu Pitts had it not been for the kindness, understanding and compassion of her high school principal. What this man did for her sets a shining example of the good that can be done by leaders who are in a position to influence the lives of others.

As a child, Zasu was unattractive, shy, awkward, skinny, and poor. The clothes she wore were hand-me-downs. She had no friends. Boys and girls alike teased her and made fun of her.

No one ever saw the tears in her eyes, not even her mother.

She walked to school and back alone and she cried alone.

To escape her drab life and the cruelty of the other children, Zasu began to dream, to create an inward world in which she was a great actress, rich and beautiful, admired by all. In her senior year in high school she visualized herself on the stage reciting *The Midnight Ride of Paul Revere.* She saw herself getting a burst of applause and showing others what a great actress she was.

She even got up the nerve to ask the principal if she could recite the poem on graduation day. Over the years, this man had befriended her, had rescued her from gangs teasing her, and inside had wept for her. He knew she would probably be hooted off the stage, but he told her that she could do it.

Zasu rehearsed in front of the mirror for weeks. It was to be her big moment, her big chance to be loved and admired. The big day finally arrived and even though she was wearing an old dress, not a new one like the other girls, she marched out on the stage confident she would win them over with her talent.

"Please, God, make me say it good. Don't let me forget my lines in the middle."

She started and there was a spontaneous burst of laughter! "Please, dear God, don't let them laugh at me." She tried again and even the teachers began to laugh. Stunned, Zasu stood on the platform, her face white. Only half finished, she bowed and walked off, dazed, hurt, and crying. "Dear God, how could you do this to me—how could you let them laugh at me that way!"

"Don't stop!" the audience yelled. "Finish it, finish it. It's the funniest thing we've ever heard!" Off stage the principal put his arm around her and said, "They love you, Zasu, go back out there and finish it!"

"They are laughing at me," she cried.

"They are laughing *with* you. They think you are wonderful.

Look here—when has the whole school ever noticed you before and really wanted you for something?"

"Want me for a laugh! For a clown!"

"What's wrong with that?" the principal challenged. "Maybe that's your mission in life. Many of us never find our place in life, Zasu. Maybe that is what God intended. His wisdom is greater than ours."

Zasu stopped crying. She could hear the audience calling for her. After all, she had prayed to God for success.

"Go on, Zasu," the principal said. "Laughter is the greatest medicine in life. It brings light into darkness, peace to aching hearts, riches that money can't buy. *Laughter is God's hand upon a troubled world.*"

Zasu Pitts returned to the stage and finished *The Midnight Ride of Paul Revere* to such applause as had never been heard in the school auditorium. The children ganged around her, congratulated her, and told her that it was the funniest thing they had ever heard.

Later in life, Zasu achieved great success and was loved all over the world. She never forgot the principal who made it all possible or the sentence that had been her lifelong inspiration: *"Laughter is God's hand upon a troubled world."*

LIKE ATTRACTS LIKE

If we are going to be happy we must learn to control worry and fear. ELIMINATE THE FEAR PICTURES you are holding in your mind. We think in pictures and every fear picture we put in our minds is like planting a BAD SEED IN FERTILE SOIL—it sprouts and grows. When we get a lot of the bad seeds planted, our minds are getting less and less good, constructive thought pictures. We then find that the things we feared have actually come to us . . . LIKE ATTRACTS LIKE!!

The Bible tells us "FOR THE THING WHICH I GREATLY FEARED IS COME UPON ME, AND THAT WHICH I WAS AFRAID OF IS COME UNTO ME." Sure, the things we fear come unto us . . . we pictured these things in our minds and used this important law to attract them.

THE LAW ALSO WORKS FOR POSITIVE RESULTS. We must SEE and PICTURE OURSELVES as the HAPPY, POSITIVE PERSON we want to be and that will come to being a reality in our life also. We must realize that if we THINK and look after our thoughts . . . then our thoughts are going to look after us by bringing us the things that we really want to achieve. PLANT BAD PICTURES, GET BAD RESULTS. PLANT GOOD PICTURES, GET GOOD RESULTS.

Learn to control your thought pictures. See yourself as the happy, successful person you want to be and you'll soon develop into that type of person. Eliminate your fear pictures! President Franklin Delano Roosevelt made this statement: "The only thing we have to fear is fear itself."

So, to be really HAPPY, we must TAKE POSSESSION of TODAY and be happy with JUST THIS ONE DAY, ONE DAY AT A TIME. Shut out the yesterdays and the tomorrows and make the most out of this very day. *The person who won't be licked, can't be licked.*

STAY BUSY

My mother is 81 years YOUNG. It's not hard to see why she is enjoying life to the fullest. She's always busy doing something constructive and never has time to sit around doing nothing. I am always amazed how she can make opportunities out of so many events in her daily life. She taught me very well the truth in this statement, "When you are killing time, you are murdering opportunity!"

At 81 she loves to fish, is always getting up a foursome to play bridge, taking care of her garden and yard, trying out new recipes, driving to various places for a "day out" . . . just never quitting. As she puts it so well, "I just don't let myself get bored—I keep on the go."

Staying busy and keeping your mind on constructive things is an excellent habit for everyone to develop to enjoy life to the fullest.

SOMETIMES WE LOSE OUR TRUE PERSPECTIVE

One morning a rancher and his wife were sitting at the breakfast table talking about all the years they had spent on the ranch. The rancher looked at his wife and said, "You know, I've lived a long time, I was born right here on this place, my father was born right here, too, and my grandfather spent many years working this land." He said, "You know what I'm going to do? I'm going to sell this ranch and we're going to move to a better place in this world."

He went to the telephone and called a real estate agent in town. He said, "I want you to come out and see me this morning. I'm going to sell my ranch." The real estate agent went out and they got into a jeep and went out to look at the ranch. They inspected every hill, every valley, and visited every corner of the property. The real estate agent said, "I think I can sell the place. I think I can get the price you want, but first I'll prepare an advertisement on this ranch and then I'll bring it out and show it to you before we put it in the paper."

In a few days he came out and they went in and spread the advertisement out on the kitchen table. It listed all of the fine things about the ranch. Together they looked it over and suddenly the rancher looked at the real estate agent and said, "You know, what I'm going to say will probably surprise you. This ranch isn't for sale at all. This describes the place I've been looking for all of my life."

Isn't it true that we sometimes lose our perspective? We FAIL to recognize and appreciate the true value of the things life has given us. Perhaps, if we stop and COUNT OUR BLESSINGS more often, we will find that things are really better than they seem and we can truly find happiness in taking possession of today.

I have done a great amount of work in the Colorado State Penitentiary. I have seen men low in morale, locked up in their cells, nothing to look forward to. I have gone through homes for the mentally retarded. I have gone through homes for the aged where some were ready for death.

When I have a tendency to get "down," all I do is say, "Grant, remember the life of the convict in his cell, the mentally retarded, the ones ready to die." Then I pick myself up real quickly by being thankful for the many good things I have and the many opportunities God gives me each day.

JUST FOR TODAY

1. Just for today I will be happy. This assumes that what Abraham Lincoln said is true, that "most folks are about as happy as they make up their minds to be." Happiness is from within; it is not a matter of externals.

2. Just for today I will try to adjust myself to what is, and not try to adjust everything to my own desires. I will take my family, my business, and my luck as they come and fit myself to them.

3. Just for today I will take care of my body. I will exercise

it, care for it, nourish it, not abuse it nor neglect it, so that it will be a perfect machine for my bidding.

4. Just for today I will try to strengthen my mind. I will learn something useful. I will not be a mental loafer. I will read something that requires effort, thought and concentration.

5. Just for today I will exercise my soul in three ways; I will do somebody a good turn and not get found out. I will do at least two things I don't want to do, as William James suggests, just for exercise.

6. Just for today I will be agreeable. I will look as well as I can, dress as becomingly as possible, talk low, act courteously, be liberal with praise, criticize not at all, nor find fault with anything and not try to regulate nor improve anyone.

7. Just for today I will try to live through this day only, not to tackle my whole life problem at once. I can do things for twelve hours that would appall me if I had to keep them up for a lifetime.

8. Just for today I will have a program. I will write down what I expect to do every hour. I may not follow it exactly, but I will have it. It will eliminate two pests, hurry and indecision.

9. Just for today I will have a quiet half-hour all by myself and relax. In this half-hour sometimes I will think of God, so as to get a little more perspective into my life.

10. Just for today I will be unafraid, especially I will not be afraid to be happy, to enjoy what is beautiful, to love, and to believe that those I love, love me.

—Sibyl F. Partridge

Resolve right now to read and reread this again and again . . . pick out one thing and PRACTICE THAT EACH DAY. It will help you to grow and to become the happy person you want to become.

YOU DON'T HAVE TO BE IN A WELL OF DEPRESSION

Old Sam was a good and faithful old mule that had helped an old farmer on the farm for many years. One morning the farmer awoke in the wee hours, wasn't able to get back to sleep, so he tossed and turned thinking about Old Sam. He finally got out of bed, put on his clothes and went out to the barn where the mule had his stall. He looked at Old Sam and said, "You know, good old friend, tomorrow I am going to turn you to the pasture, you are going to retire. All you'll have to do is eat and sleep from tomorrow morning on." Then the farmer went back to bed.

As soon as the sun rose in the east he got up, dressed and took Old Sam out to the pasture. There he removed the halter, slapped the mule on the side and turned him loose to graze. During the next few days the farmer would see the mule from time to time, but suddenly one day the mule turned up missing.

The farmer searched the pasture from end to end and side to side, but nowhere was Old Sam to be found. It occurred to the farmer that he hadn't looked down the old abandoned well which had become overgrown with grass and weeds and was located way down in the pasture's southwest corner.

He immediately went there and sure enough, there was Old Sam standing down in the bottom of the well switching his tail back and forth. This presented the farmer with quite a problem . . . he didn't want to let the old mule starve to death in the bottom of the well and yet he didn't know how to get him out either. After much thought the farmer decided to get a shovel and began throwing dirt into the well to bury Old Sam right there. Each shovelful would land on the mule's back, but instead of just standing there, the mule would shake off the dirt and then stand on it. Shovelful after shovelful of dirt would land on Old Sam's back, but he would shake it off, step up and stand on it. A few hours later the dirt pile approached the top of the well and Old Sam just stepped out and went down the pasture eating grass and switching his tail.

ADVERSITY, FEAR, WORRY, FAILURE comes to all of us and we can find ourselves in a well of depression . . . but we have a choice. We can stand still in our WELL OF DEPRES-SION, be overwhelmed and do nothing about it or we can shake it off and RISE ABOVE IT. The choice is ours.

Two men get fired from a job. One man will go home and tell his wife and be in a well of depression for a month or maybe longer. The other man goes home and tells his wife, "Honey, guess what? I just got fired from my job. It's the best thing that ever happened to me." Again, the choice is up to us.

ARE YOU LETTING WHAT YOU DON'T HAVE DESTROY WHAT YOU DO HAVE?

God has given every one of us the potential to be a very happy person. Too much of the time we are so busy keeping our minds on the little beetles of life, the things that are wrong, the bad, the negatives, wishing we had this or that, and complaining about things, that we DESTROY all of the many GOOD THINGS that we do have. Yes, most people are as happy as they make up their minds to be!

▲   ▲   ▲   ▲

"GARDLINES" *by Grant G. Gard*

DON'T TALK ABOUT THESE THINGS—DO THEM NOW!!

1. Think HAPPINESS.
2. Build only STRONG, POSITIVE MENTAL PICTURES of your-

self being the happy person you really want to be.

3. Don't PUT OFF living in the distant future.
4. Don't live your life reaching the end with an empty basket.
5. Make ADVERSITIES the OPPORTUNITY to become an even better person.
6. Don't carry worries and fears to your job or let them destroy your home life.
7. Never allow yourself to live in a WELL OF DEPRESSION.
8. LAUGH more and lighten the burden of TENSION, FEAR and WORRY.
9. Don't lose your PERSPECTIVE—recognize and appreciate the true value of the life God has given you.
10. Be determined to ACT like the happy person you really want to be. The feeling will soon be there.
11. Be determined NEVER to let fear keep you from doing what you want to do.
12. LOVE what you do.
13. STAY BUSY.

▲　▲　▲　▲

Thought Provoking Quotes

"Worry is the interest paid by those who borrow trouble."
　　　　　　　—*George Washington Lyon*

"The difference between concern and worry is a stomach ulcer."
　　　　　　　—*Grand G. Gard*

"Never submit your mind to a dead sheet of paper."
　　　　　　　—*Bishop Fulton Sheen*

"We go about partially killing ourselves when we lose the present worry by worrying about the irretrievable past and the unpredictable future."

　　　　　　　—*Peter J. Steincrohn*
　　　　　(*How to Stop Killing Yourself*—Funk)

"If a man loses his reverence for any part of life, he will lose his reverence for all of life."

—Albert Schweitzer

"To live is the rarest thing in the world—most people exist—that is all."

—Oscar Wilde

"A man may fail many times, but he won't be a failure until he says that someone pushed him."

—Elmer G. Leterman

"Maturity is the ability to do a job whether you're supervised or not; finish a job once it's started; carry money without spending it and last, but not least, the ability to bear an injustice without wanting to get even."

—Fred S. Cook

"Happy the man, and happy he alone
He, who can call today his own—
He who secure within can say—
Tomorrow, do thy worst for I have lived today."

—Horace

"The confidence which we have in ourselves gives birth to much of that which we have in others."

—Francois de la Rochfeaucauld

"Two people who love each other are in a place more holy than the interior of a church."

—William Lyon Phelps

"Love is strong as death—many waters can not quench love, neither can the floods drown it."

—Song of Solomon 8:6, 7

"Live for the day only, and for the day's work—the chief worries of life arise from the foolish habit of looking before and after."

—Sir William Osler

"The sovereign cure for worry is prayer."
—William James

9 | *Creating an Acceptance Climate for Yourself and Your Ideas*

All of us want two things out of life: SUCCESS and HAPPINESS. All of us are different. Your idea of success may be different from mine. But I can assure you there is ONE BIG FACTOR which all of us must learn to deal with if we are going to be successful and/or happy. The BIG FACTOR is the same regardless of your profession, be it lawyer, farmer, doctor, business person, sales person, housewife or whatever.

The one common denominator to all success and happiness is OTHER PEOPLE!

Many studies have clearly shown that if you learn how to work and deal with other people, you will have gone about 85% down the road to success in any business, profession or occupation, and at the same time about 99.99 per cent of the way down the road to personal happiness.

WHERE SUCCESS AND HAPPINESS COME FROM

Look around you. Are the most successful people you know those with the most brains, the most skill? Are the people who are the happiest and get the most fun out of life so much smarter than the other people you know? If you will really stop and think a minute, the chances are that you will come to the conclusion that the people you know who are the most successful, and enjoy life the most, are those who HAVE A WAY WITH OTHER PEOPLE.

SUCCESS . . . 15% TECHNICAL . . . 85% PEOPLE

The Carnegie Institute of Technology analyzed the records of 10,000 persons and arrived at the conclusion that 15 per cent of success is due to technical training, to brains and skill on the job, and 85 percent of success is due to personality factors, to ability to deal with people successfully!

The percentage ran even higher in a study reported by Dr. Albert Edward Wiggam, in his syndicated column, "Let's Explore Your Mind." Out of 4,000 persons who lost their jobs in one year, only 10 per cent or 400 lost out because they could not do their work. Ninety per cent, or 3,600 of them, lost out because they had not developed the personality to successfully deal with other people.

When the Bureau of Vocational Guidance at Harvard University made a study of thousands of men and women who had been fired, they found that for every one person who lost a job for failure to do the work, two persons lost their jobs for failure to deal successfully with people!

Regardless of our occupation, WE ARE IN THE PEOPLE BUSINESS!

CREATE A FAVORABLE ACCEPTANCE CLIMATE

In order to create a good first impression and create an acceptance climate for ourselves and our ideas, we must think, act, and talk in such as way that other people: RESPECT US, TRUST US, LIKE US, BELIEVE US, and ADMIRE US. Those are FIVE KEY AREAS.

You have only one opportunity to make a good first impression. If the first impression is not favorable, you may never recover the confidence of the people around you. A BAD IMPRESSION is almost impossible to overcome, whether it is made when we first meet someone or if it is made 30 minutes, 3 days or 3 months later. You may spend several hours, days or weeks trying to overcome one bad first impression, or a bad impression that was made later, and never be successful in gaining "acceptance."

NO ONE HAS EVER HAD A SECOND CHANCE TO CHANGE A BAD FIRST IMPRESSION. People are quick to judge. An impression, be it good or bad, is made in the first few seconds after meeting someone. The eyes of other people are upon us. Their eyes are just like a camera. The shutter goes closed. Is the image favorable or unfavorable? That picture is in another's mind for a long, long time. Did the picture they took of us gain their respect, trust, make them believe us, like us and admire us? Better be sharp and quick in thinking, saying and doing the right things.

Here are some ideas that I know are of uppermost importance in creating an ACCEPTANCE CLIMATE for you and your ideas. These are very basic ideas, but it is the "basics" that move people ahead.

HAVE FUN DOING IT . . . If we have fun and enjoy our work, the feeling and action will rub off. We'll transmit this feeling to other people. Remember, we said part of being a successful businessperson, manager, leader, salesperson or parent is making others feel as we feel about our ideas, concepts or products. If we are not having fun and enjoying our work, others will know this and we will not be very successful. If YOU are not having fun in YOUR work, then it's time for you to find something new to do because you are paying too big a price. You are doing an injustice to yourself, the company you represent or work for, your profession and your family.

Many people unknowlingly create a bad impression because they don't realize that a person is judged not only by the value that person puts on himself, but they are judged also by the value put on other things such as a job. You yourself are more responsible for how you are accepted than anyone else. FEW PEOPLE REALIZE THAT THE WORLD FORMS ITS OPINION OF US LARGELY FROM THE OPINION WE HAVE OF OURSELVES. I'm saying *Have a good self-image* and *just be yourself.* The people who do this are the people who love and enjoy their work and their life.

Act as if you are a NOBODY and the world will take you at your own value. Act as if you are SOMEBODY and the world has no choice but to treat you as SOMEBODY. It's that RIGHT feeling on the INSIDE that produces that RIGHT image on the OUTSIDE.

I have a good friend in Dr. George Bridges of Lawton, Oklahoma. One of the reasons he is very successful as a dentist is his ability to enjoy what he is doing and to have lots of fun doing it. You can tell by his actions and feelings that every patient is something new to him and that he can hardly wait to help. He thoroughly enjoys his work and his patients know it. He is building all the clientele he can handle. He, like most Pros, would say "I never worked a day in my life . . . it's all been so much fun."

Dr. Bridges has got everything going for him on the "inside" and it all shows up in a positive way on the "outside".

SMILE

A simple smile helps us to create an ACCEPTANCE CLIMATE. It takes more muscles to frown than it does to smile and a smile means so much more. Perhaps we had better check to see if we are radiating happiness. Many people will say that they don't always feel like smiling. My reply to that is that a FORCED SMILE is much better than a SINCERE FROWN!

A smile helps to CREATE THE RIGHT IMAGE and a smile on your face even when you are talking on the telephone helps to create the right image even though it can't be seen.

I know of one company that required the PBX operators to look into a mirror and smile before they said anything on the phone just so they would create the right image on the phone through their voices.

My attorney, Richard E. Hartman of Denver, and his lovely wife, Rhondda, never will want for friends and clients. They are expert human engineers and always wear big, likeable smiles. They are as beautiful on the INSIDE as they are on the OUTSIDE.

A smile says, "I LIKE YOU" and people love that kind of attitude.

TAKE A SINCERE INTEREST IN OTHERS

People aren't going to care about us until they first know how much we care about them. You can never become truly rich except by enriching the lives of others. You will never truly prosper unless you bring prosperity to others.

Kettering put it so well when he said, "Before I accept or

buy an idea, a product or service, I first must buy the integrity, the enthusiasm, and the dedication of the person offering me that idea, service, or product."

Many people stand over the stove saying, "STOVE, GIVE ME HEAT". They aren't willing to put the coal and wood in the fire to make the heat. Too many people have the "GIVE ME" attitude, rather than the "GIVE OUT" attitude. You must put the fuel in the stove first; the fuel of doing the right things right; the fuel of taking a sincere interest in others; the fuel of good human engineering principles; and then, and only then, will you receive the heat from the stove . . . the heat being the rewards of life.

How do you measure your interest in others? It's easy . . . your income is the measure of your service to others.

Before a person keeps a cow or a chicken around that cow has to produce meat or milk and a chicken has to lay eggs, but we gladly keep a dog around and see to it that he is fed well and has a nice place to sleep just for wagging his tail and for taking a sincere interest in us.

Why should people be interested in us until they first know how much we are interested in them?

Don't fake it—be genuine. Nothing is going to take the place of sincerity. It's the quality that all really successful people have and it stems from having the "I REALLY CARE ABOUT YOU" attitude. SINCERITY is the key that opens the hearts and minds of people.

SINCERITY is genuine, it's real . . . INSINCERITY is like counterfeit money; if we pass it long enough it's going to get us into trouble!

People respond to people who are sincerely interested in them. WE ARE REPULSED BY THE INSINCERE, ARTIFICIAL SWEET MASSAGE OF OUR EGO . . . the one who tries to spread it on with a trowel just to get something for himself.

I can't tell you *how* to be sincere. It has to come from within. I can tell you what causes a person to be sincere and that is this: You must have a "heartfelt" desire to help people and you must have the "I really care about you" attitude. Sincerity comes from the heart—insincerity comes just from the lips. In fact, that has been called "lip service". It is amazing what can and does happen when we forget ourselves and think only of other people and what we can do to help others solve their problems.

People only want to know what we can do for them. William J. Reilly, Ph.D., author and consultant to major companies in the field of human relations, once said, "We are always in danger of telling others much more about ourselves than they are interested in knowing." To illustrate this point Dr. Reilly related the following story . . . "Not long ago I attended a conference in which a brilliant young inventor explained his latest brain child to some financiers. Their minds were open. *They* had asked for the meeting. It was an important meeting for this young inventor. It was his big chance. The men he was talking to had the money and the connections to put his invention over.

"We arrived at his workshop shortly before noon. The inventor began by dwelling on the exhilarating conception, the painful birth, and the expensive development of his big idea. From there he went on and on with endless figures and charts.

"At ten minutes after two, one of the financiers exploded. 'Look'! he interrupted the inventor, 'we've been listening to you for over two hours. You've led us into the jungle of your scientific adventures, pointed out every difficulty—every single dark cave you've gotten yourself into and you've explained in detail how you finally fought your way out. And we're still not out of the woods. I *still* don't know what you've got or what it'll do for *me*!'

"'I'm coming to that,' assured the inventor. 'But you men don't know what I've been through.'

"'Look,' the financier interrupted again, 'people are not interested in processes. People are interested only in results. People will never know what *you've been through*. People don't care. That's the secret cross you'll have to bear alone. People don't give a hoot how difficult it was for you to arrive at something worthwhile. *They only want to know what it will do for them.*'"

So to create an ACCEPTANCE CLIMATE for yourself and your ideas, take a sincere interest, tell people what you can do for them, don't bore them with your personal events and facts that they aren't interested in.

BE PUNCTUAL

God forbid, the person who doesn't make a practice of being on time in everything he does! I have seen many people continually late for civic meetings, company meetings, appointments, luncheon engagements, etc. This reflects a POOR ATTITUDE, LACK OF RESPECT, LACK OF ORGANIZATION and LACK OF GOOD WORKING HABITS. You can't expect to create an acceptance climate when you are not showing other people the respect they deserve.

RESPECT PEOPLE

Napoleon and a lady were walking down a path when they met some workmen carrying heavy loads. The lady ordered them to make way for Napoleon, but he interrupted her saying, "*Respect the burden, Madame, always respect the man with a burden.*"

It's a well known fact . . . in order to gain respect *from* people you must show respect *to* people.

MAKE PEOPLE FEEL IMPORTANT

The deepest craving we all have, and it's one that must be satisfied, is the feeling to be IMPORTANT, to feel WANTED and to feel APPRECIATED. We must be able to fulfill this craving in others and do it honestly and sincerely. Make it a habit of LOOKING FOR THE GOOD IN PEOPLE—NOT THE BAD. Making people feel important should be part of your everyday life. Make it one of your POSITIVE HABITS. Look for the good in people and tell them. BUILD PEOPLE ON THEIR STRENGTHS and the WEAKNESSES will, most of the time, take care of themselves. It is a human engineering skill on which most of our happiness and success depends.

"Talk to a man about himself," said Disraeli, one of the shrewdest men who ever ruled the British Empire, "talk to a man about himself and he will listen for hours."

That is the art of good human relations, an art on which volumes have been written. Yet the whole subject can be condensed into one sentence, "The only way to live happily with people is to overlook their faults and admire their virtues." Show everyone real, sincere appreciation and praise.

When with pleasure you are viewing
Something that a man is doing
And you like him or love him
Tell him Now.
Don't withhold your approbation
Til the preacher makes oration
And he lies with snowy lilies on his brow.

For no matter how you shout'eth
He won't really care about it,
 And he won't know how many teardrops you have shed.
So if you think some praise is due him,
 Now's the time to slip it to him,
Because he can't read his tombstone when he's dead.

—Unknown

Make everyone you come in contact with every day feel that they are the most important person on the face of this earth, praise them honestly and sincerely, and you'll create a real *acceptance climate* for yourself and you'll be known as a *genuine people builder*.

If you doubt that people like to feel important, stop and analyze yourself. When a group picture comes out and your picture is in it . . . whose picture do you look for first? If the newspaper is carrying an article about you, what's the first thing you do? You skip the international news, the state news and get right down to the local news to see your name in print. EVERYONE LIKES TO FEEL IMPORTANT.

Charles Schwab was paid a million dollars a year by Andrew Carnegie. When Schwab was asked why he was able to earn this large salary his reply was, "I consider my ability to arouse enthusiasm among men the greatest asset I possess, and the way to develop the best that is in a man is by appreciation and encouragement. There is nothing else that so kills the ambitions of a man as criticism from his superiors. I never criticize anyone. I believe in giving a man incentive to work. So I am anxious to praise and loath to find fault. If I like anything, I am hearty in my approbation and lavish in my praise."

He further stated, "In my wide association in life, meeting with many and great men in various parts of the world, I have yet to find the man, however great or exalted his station, who did not do better work and put forth greater effort under the spirit of approval than he would ever do under the spirit of criticism."

Charles Fillmore said, "The whole creation responds to praise and is glad. Animal trainers pet and reward their charges with delicacies for acts of obedience; children glow with joy and gladness when they are praised".

Always look for the good things in other people that you can praise and let people know the good things that you see. Also, look for the good things in your own life instead of the bad, the negative.

Pay sincere compliments. Never underestimate the power of praise and a sincere compliment. The story is told of the janitor who worked many years for a company by cleaning offices. Since his hours were midnight to 8 A.M. he rarely saw his employer. One morning, however, his boss came to the office early and spotting the janitor in the hall called him into his office. Fearing the worst, the janitor slowly walked up to the desk. "John," his boss began, "I just wanted to tell you how much I appreciate your very fine work. My desk and our offices are always so neat and clean. It's a pleasure to come to work each day. Thank you so much for doing such a fine job."

The janitor didn't say a word, just nodded his head, turned and left. Shortly afterwards there was a light knock on the office door. "Come in," said the boss. It was John, standing there holding his hat. Fumbling for words he said, "I just want to say, Sir, that in all the years I've worked here that's the first time anyone has noticed my work. Thank you very much. I appreciate your compliment as much as your signature on my pay check."

Praise and compliments must be specific and sincere. People have a natural need to feel that they are wanted and that their efforts are appreciated. Sincere praise and compliments fill this need. With praise . . . people try harder to do their best because they *want to*. With criticism . . . if they try harder, it's because they *have to*.

Start right at home with your wife, husband, children and then your friends, associates and clients. Instead of saying, "That was a fine meal." Say something like this: "That was certainly a well-cooked meal, the chicken was browned and crisped to perfection" . . . or instead of "That is a good-looking suit you have on," say, "That is certainly a stylish suit you are wearing, that blue tie really brings out the best in the suit."

In Dorothy Dix's newspaper column she claimed that she was tired of always hearing lectures to brides. She thought it was time to give the bridegroom some advice and here's what she wrote:

"Never get married until you have kissed the Blarney Stone. Praising a woman before marriage is a matter of inclination. But praising one after you marry her is a matter of necessity—and personal safety. Matrimony is no place for candor. It is a field for diplomacy.

"If you wish to fare sumptuously every day, never knock your wife's housekeeping or make invidious comparisons between it and your mother's. But, on the contrary, be forever praising her domesticity and openly congratulate yourself upon having married the only woman who combines the attractions of Venus and Minerva and Mary Ann. Even when the steak is leather and the bread a cinder, don't complain. Merely remark that the meal isn't up to her usual standard of perfection, and she will make a burnt offering of herself on the kitchen stove to live up to your ideal of her."

I ask you, "Why not bring her some flowers or a box of candy?" You'll say, "Yes, I ought to do it." *Don't Talk About It—DO IT.*

RETURN A COMPLIMENT WITH A COMPLIMENT! So many times we say something like this after we receive a compliment: "Gee, I don't deserve that," or something to that effect. Really, we are saying that the person was wrong in giving us the compliment. So try something like this: "Thank you for the lovely compliment, coming from a person in your position, that really means a great deal." You make the other person feel good and important, also.

Give people a good name. A midwest farmer had a hired hand named George. Though a good worker most of the time, George was an independent, unpredictable man.

One morning he came down to the barn and announced that he didn't feel like plowing that day. The farmer did not compel the hired man to get busy, though the fields did need plowing immediately. Instead he expressed sympathy and concern over the condition of his health. He urged George to go to the house and get back into bed.

The hired man listened in silence and made no move to return to the house. The farmer explained that he didn't have anyone who could plow as straight a furrow as George, and that he certainly didn't know how he could get along without him. He was too good a man not to be missed. So would he please go back to the house and rest. The sooner he got well, the sooner he could return to the plowing.

Still the hired man hung around the barn. The farmer went off to finsh some chores and, upon his return, acted surprised to see the man still there. Again, he urged him to return to the house and go to bed. He was too valuable a man to be sick and he wanted him to get well just as soon as possible. He explained that he did not want to send another man out to do George's job because no one could do the job as well as he could.

A few minutes later George mumbled something about feeling

better and guessed he'd go out and plow. All day long he plowed, whistling at his job, and cutting every furrow just as neatly as he possibly could.

DRESS LIKE A SUCCESS

I have heard a lot of debates on dress. One top-notch executive gave me some of the wisest advice I have ever received about the clothes we wear. He said, "Dress so that you create the RIGHT IMAGE and are COMFORTABLE in front of the HIGHEST TYPE CLIENT you might be talking to that day." I have seen way too many leaders, executives and salespeople dress in a sloppy manner; pants not pressed; shoes not shined; hair not combed; and even some, in this day and age, have B.O.

Buy good clothes. Go to a good, reputable clothing store and ask for advice. Tell them what you do. Ask them what to wear to help you create an ACCEPTANCE CLIMATE for yourself so that you can always function at your best. I've always said, "Don't be the very first one to wear the latest change of style, but for sure, don't be the last one either."

Good clothes will cost more, but in the long run, they won't cost as much because they will last longer. There is absolutely no doubt in my mind that good clothes help to create the RIGHT IMAGE and help to BUILD SELF-CONFIDENCE so that you can THINK, ACT, AND TALK like a WINNER. Good clothes help you to FEEL SUCCESSFUL and to RADIATE SUCCESS.

CONFIDENCE BREEDS CONFIDENCE

Many people of mediocre ability get farther ahead than others who have outstanding talents for the simple reason they know how to act with confidence.

As was brought out in Chapter 6 . . . You can make others around you enthusiastic by your being enthusiastic. You can also make others have confidence in you by your acting confidently.

In his early years, Conrad Hilton had far more confidence than money. About all he had for assets was a reputation for keeping his word and the ability to inspire in others the same confidence in his plans that he felt himself. No matter the problems and obstacles, Hilton always acted as if it were impossible to fail. This very manner worked like magic inspiring others to believe he could not fail.

His first hotel was begun with less than $50,000 of his own money. When his mother came upon him drawing plans and asked what he was doing, he told her he was planning a really big hotel.

"Where will the money come from?" she asked. "In here," said Hilton, pointing toward his head. He had exhausted every possible source and succeeded in raising only about a half million dollars in capital. The architects gave him an estimate for the hotel he wanted to build and said it would cost at least one million dollars. Without any hesitation, he said, "Draw up the plans."

Hilton then actually began building the hotel without having the slightest idea where the money was going to come from to finish it. In summary, because he himself not only talked of building a million dollar hotel, but actually acted as if he meant to do it, other people became convinced that Conrad Hilton *could* do it and they invested their money.

Henry Ford financed his company in its early days largely through using a confident manner. He had his back to the wall more than once, but by acting as if he could not fail, he inspired others with this same confidence.

John D. Rockefeller used the same technique. When a creditor came calling and wanted his bill paid, Rockefeller would reach for his checkbook and say, "Which would you rather have, cash or Standard Oil stock?'' He appeared so calm and confident that nearly all decided to take stock in his company and none ever lived to regret it.

Complete knowledge builds confidence. You must earn the confidence of other people and this means know 20 or 30 times as much about your idea, concept, product as you can use in conversing with other people.

The president of a large rubber company was making a speech. After he finished, a young man said, "Would it be too personal if I asked you how you got to be president of this big company?"

"Not at all," the president replied. "I was working in a filling station and not making much progress. One day I read that if a person wanted to get ahead he must know all there was to know about his particular business or product. So, on one of my vacations, I went back to the home office and watched them make rubber tires. I'd watch them put in the nylon cords. On one vacation I went to Africa to watch them plant the rubber trees and even extract the base of the crude rubber. So when I was asked about my product, I didn't say, 'This is what I think.' No, I said, 'This is what I know. I was there. I watched them put those nylon cords in to make the finest tire ever made, to protect your family against blow-outs. I watched them extract that crude rubber to make the finest tire in the world.' "

He then said, "There is no force in the world that has a greater impact than the statement of a knowledgeable person fortified by confidence and experience."

People who know, and know that they know, can speak with authority that has no comparison. The world makes way for people who know what they are doing and have EARNED THE RIGHT to be doing the thing that they are doing.

Others will have confidence in us in direct proportion to the amount of confidence we have in ourselves.

In creating an ACCEPTANCE CLIMATE you must be completely convinced and dedicated to the idea, concept or product you want to get across. When you are sold, and the other person *knows you are sold,* he'll want it.

BE A GOOD LISTENER

LISTEN carefully to everything that is said. Many people think they have to do all the talking to be a good conversationalist, but this is NOT TRUE. Get people started talking about their likes and interests. LISTEN and they'll think you are a good conversationalist.

I know of one manager in Oklahoma City who could be a first-rate man if he would just learn to listen and analyze what people are saying. Instead, about the time a person gets half way through what he is saying, this man butts in and thinks that he has all the answers. He doesn't even know what the problem is because he won't show the other person enough respect to let him finish what he has to say.

To be good listeners, we must turn our *receiver on* and *shut off our transmitter.*

Here are some important points to practice in order to become a good listener:

1. Take a sincere interest in what the other person is saying.
   Occasionally agree, nod, smile.
2. Look directly at the other person.
   Don't look at the floor or ceiling but directly into his or her eyes.
3. Never, never interrupt.
   Show respect and show the common courtesy of hearing the other person out without any interruptions.
4. Ask questions.

This lets the person know you are interested and listening.

5. Quote the other person from time to time.

The other person will know that you have listened if you occasionally say, "As you said"; "As you pointed out so well"; or "I like your remark and the way you brought out. . . ."

6. Don't change subjects.

Stay with one subject until the conversation is finalized.

7. Keep your emotions under control.

Stay calm and cool, be the positive, stabilizing influence.

Justice Oliver Wendell Holmes was asked the secret of his success. He replied, "To be able to listen to others in a sympathetic and understanding manner is perhaps the most effective mechanism in the world for getting along with people and tying up their friendship for good. Too few people practice the 'white magic' of being good listeners."

DON'T ARGUE AND BECOME ANGRY

I was working in a little town in Iowa and a very successful insurance man told me of an incident that had just happened to him. A farmer had a claim. This man had written the insurance and had a claim adjuster call on the farmer. The farmer felt the claim adjuster had been very UNFAIR and the settlement was not at all satisfactory.

The farmer immediately drove to town to tell the agent off. His face was "red" with anger. He walked in and "unloaded" on the agent. The agent told me, "I just stood there and listened. I knew if I would say anything, it would be wrong, so I let him go all the way through until he was finished and then I said, 'Bill, you are real important to me and a good customer, I want to get all the facts straight. Would you please tell me all of the story ONE MORE TIME so I can make IMPORTANT NOTES!' "

Yes, by the time the farmer had gone through the story once more, the agent did not ARGUE and become ANGRY. He listened and made the farmer feel important and the farmer cooled down. They could then figure out a more reasonable settlement which was acceptable to both parties. LISTENING is the key, not arguing and being angry.

Anger is often more harmful than the injury that caused it. When Leonardo da Vinci was working on his painting "The Last Supper," he became angry with a certain man. Losing his temper, he lashed the other fellow with bitter words and threats. Returning to his canvas he attempted to work on the face of Jesus, but was unable to do so. He was so upset he could not compose himself for the painstaking work. Finally he put down his tools and sought out the man and asked his forgiveness. The man accepted his apology and Leonardo was able to return to his workshop and finish painting the face of Jesus.

You can't win an argument. As wise old Ben Franklin said, "If you argue and rankle and contradict, you may achieve a victory sometimes; but it will be an empty victory because you will never get your opponent's good will."

You can't win an argument. You can't, because if you lose it, you lose it; and if you win it, you lose it! Why? Even if you win it you have probably made the other person feel very inferior. You have hurt the other person's pride and your triumph will be resented.

> "A man convinced against his will
> Is of the same opinion still."

The *Boston Transcript* once printed this clever bit of sound advice:

"Here lies the body of William Jay
Who died maintaining his right of way
He was right, dead right, as he sped along
But he's just as dead as if he were wrong."

You can be dead right in your argument but as far as changing the other person's mind is concerned, you will never do it and maintain any kind of positive relationship with him again.

Look at the other person's point of view. A trapper and a storekeeper had quite a profitable relationship. The trapper bartered all of his furs to the storekeeper. The storekeeper provided the trapper with all of his supplies. Late one evening, the trapper and the storekeeper sat next to the fire recounting to each other the day's events.

"Ran into the smartest darn squirrel I ever saw," said the trapper. "Fast little devil, too. Had him trapped against a tree . . . drew a bead on him, but just before I fired, he moved around the tree."

"Well, I moved to the right and he moved to the left. Then I went the other way and he went the other way. I ran circles around the squirrel and never did get a shot at him. Never got him in a position where I could see him and he couldn't see me."

The storekeeper looked at him for a moment and said, "No. You didn't. You didn't run around the squirrel. You couldn't have run around the squirrel."

A "did too" . . . "did not" . . . heated argument ensued. It got louder and louder until finally the trapper could stand no more and walked out, never to trade again with the storekeeper.

Both the trapper and the storekeeper were right, but this silly argument ruined a friendship and a business relationship. IT SIMPLY DEPENDS ON YOUR POINT OF VIEW. The trapper, of course, was using the tree as his point of reference. He ran around the tree—the squirrel was on the tree—therefore he ran around the squirrel. The storekeeper naturally saw it differently. He used the squirrel as his point of reference and since the trapper never got into a position where the squirrel had his back to him, he couldn't have possibly run around the squirrel.

A profitable business relationship was completely destroyed simply because neither person could see the other's point of view.

My point is this . . . ALWAYS put yourself in the other person's shoes and look out of his eyes. *Use empathy in all of your dealings with people.* A real pro always tries to see things from the other person's point of view.

CALL PEOPLE BY NAME

Another way to create an ACCEPTANCE CLIMATE is by developing the ability to CALL PEOPLE BY THEIR NAME. (See Chapter 15)

NO ROOM FOR GLOOM

Negative talk and negative opinions give a bad impression. People just simply don't want to be around the chronic complainer . . . the type of person who has a mental recession going on in between his ears at all times.

I saw one fellow on an airplane flight who looked so down, so depressed and so sour that you would have sworn we were all passengers in a Goodyear blimp who had just looked out the window and had seen a woodpecker fly by!! It's going to crash!!

Logically, things cannot be bad or wrong ALL of the time— even a stopped clock is right twice every 24 hours.

But that's the way it is with a lot of people. Remember, I said, "What's around you, is you." By being gloomy, depressed and negative you actually create a negative mood all around you.

Don't expect to get a "yes" or "favorable" response from other people if you have set a "negative state."

If you give the impression that your company isn't very much, your community isn't very much, your product isn't very much, your church isn't very much then others will think that you can't be very much yourself or you wouldn't be associated with such a thing or doing what you are doing. *Simply stated, pessimistic, gloomy, negative people do not build a positive acceptance climate.*

Always be and act busy. People like to work for and do business with a positive, busy person. The person who gets to the top in his or her field does not waste valuable time and is far too busy accomplishing set goals to be boring people and wasting the time of others with "Gloom and Doom."

LIFT AND BUILD PEOPLE—DON'T PUSH

Lifting and building people up to our PLATEAU OF EXCITEMENT should be another goal we have in dealing with people. PEOPLE HATE TO BE PUSHED. In order to lift and build people to our plateau of excitement, we have to be exicted about the opportunity of working with people, working in our job and promoting our product.

But there is one other thing that I have found that is a *MUST to be a true lifter and builder of people.* In addition to being excited and practicing good human relations, WE HAVE TO LIKE OURSELVES! *We cannot lift and build people if we don't like the person we see in the mirror.*

THE GUY IN THE GLASS

When you get what you want in your struggle for self
And the world makes you king for a day,
Then go to the mirror and look at yourself
And see what that guy has to say.

For it isn't your mother, your father or wife
Whose judgment on you must pass.
The fellow whose verdict counts most in your life
Is the guy staring back from the glass.

He's the fellow to please, nevermind all the rest.
For he's with you clean to the end;
And you've passed your most dangerous and difficult test
If the guy in the glass is your friend.

You may be like Jack Horner and chisel a plum
And think you are a wonderful guy,
But the guy in the glass says you are a bum
If you can't look him straight in the eye.

You may fool the whole world—down the pathway of years
And get pats on the back as you pass;
But the final reward will be heartaches and tears
If you've cheated the guy in the glass.

                                   —Anonymous

LIKE AND ACCEPT YOURSELF

In order to lift and build others, you have to be able to lift and build yourself into the type of person you want to be and do the things you want to do.

You have to ACCEPT YOURSELF. There's only ONE YOU and be GLAD YOU ARE YOU. You also have to FORGET YOURSELF and keep your mind on the positive results of what you can do for others. In order to lift and build people, you have to GET TOTALLY INVOLVED with people and their problems and what you can do to help solve them.

Too many people fail to forget themselves and forget to get involved. It's really not difficult to lift and build people to new highs if you just start looking for the good in them and the good in yourself.

A nurse once told me that she was having real problems getting along with other people. She started analyzing and found out that she didn't like herself and consequently other people disturbed her. When she changed her attitude about herself and lifted herself up out of the doldrums, she said that everything began to change.

I said earlier that when the man was right, the world was right. That nurse began to be a lifter of people and builder of people because she had lifted herself to NEW HIGHS and began to see herself as a NEW, DYNAMIC PERSON. Think of yourself on a high level. Create and visualize that dynamic person you really want to be. Like and accept yourself and you, too, can be a lifter and a builder of people.

THE KISS OF DEATH

In dealing with people, never say, "I AM GOING TO PROVE" . . . that's one of the worst things you can ever say and yet, I hear people say it on occasion.

Be smarter than other people in your field. AS A PROFESSIONAL, YOU SHOULD BE THE EXPERT. Use tact when a difference of opinion comes up . . . NEVER ARGUE. Say something like this, "I may be wrong, but let's examine the record and see what it shows" . . . or . . . "I thought the same way until I took this into consideration" . . . or . . . "Let's take a closer look."

If you say, "By golly, I'll prove it to you." You are really saying that you are smarter than they are and that is bad because you are slapping them down.

Be smarter than the other person, but do not come right out

and say so. Be gracious, use tact and obtain your desired results through GOOD HUMAN RELATIONS TECHNIQUES. A good Human Relationist lifts and builds people to his or her level and creates a FAVORABLE ACCEPTANCE CLIMATE.

▲ ▲ ▲ ▲

"GARDLINES" *by Grant G. Gard*

DON'T TALK ABOUT THESE THINGS—DO THEM NOW!!

1. Be determined to have FUN doing your job—if you can't, the price is too high.
2. SMILE—It takes more muscles to frown than it does to SMILE and a smile means so much more.
3. Buy the BEST CLOTHES you can. Be determined to be known as a good dresser.
4. BE PUNCTUAL.
5. Be a GOOD LISTENER.
6. Take a SINCERE INTEREST in people.
7. Be determined to obtain and dig up everything about your profession so that you EARN THE CONFIDENCE of others.
8. Call people by NAME . . . work on this one, it is very important.
9. Be determined to pay SINCERE COMPLIMENTS and give SINCERE APPRECIATION for the good things people do for you or you see them doing for others.
10. Look for the GOOD in people, overlook the BAD.
11. LIFT AND BUILD PEOPLE to your plateau of EXCITE-MENT—Don't push people . . . they'll push back.
12. Lift and build yourself to new HIGH PLATEAUS.
13. ALWAYS create an ACCEPTANCE CLIMATE whereby people respect, trust, like, believe and admire you.
14. Don't allow "ROOM FOR GLOOM."
15. Try to see things from ANOTHER'S POINT OF VIEW.
16. Give people a GOOD NAME.

17. Make people feel IMPORTANT and do it with SINCERITY.
18. Control others by adopting the ATTITUDE, ACTION and FEEL-INGS that you want others to have.
19. Talk about the other persons' INTERESTS.

THOUGHT PROVOKING QUOTES

"You give but little when you give of your possessions, it is when you give of yourself that you truly give."

—Kahil Gibram

"More important than the knowledge of outer space is the possession of inner peace."

—Unknown

"To love someone is to bid him to live—to invite him to GROW."

—Unknown

"A true critic ought to dwell rather upon a person's excellencies than imperfections."

—Addison

"It isn't the business you get. It's the business you hold that counts."

—Bruce Crowell

"If you want to get the work done—ask the busy man. The other kind has no time."

—E. Hubbard

"Little pots soon run over."
—Dutch Proverb

"We are what we repeatedly do. Excellence, then, is not an act but a habit."

—Aristotle

"Those who have the largest hearts have the soundest understanding; and he is the truest philosopher who can forget himself."

—William Hazlitt

"Heaven never helps the man who will not act."
—Sophocles

"Circumstances! I make circumstances."
—Napoleon

"It's easier to be critical than correct."
—Edward R. Murrow

"To love and win is the best thing, to love and lose the next best."
—William M. Thackery

"Lack of time is an excuse, not a reason. We find the time for anything we really want to do."

—Unknown

"How much time he gains who does not look to see what his neighbor says or does or thinks."

—Marcus Aurelius

"The most exhausting thing in life is being insincere."
—Anne Morrow Lindbergh

"Since thou art not sure of a minute, throw not away an hour."
—Benjamin Franklin

10 | *Breaking Mental Barriers*

Have you placed chains of restraint on yourself? Dickens said, "*We* forge the chains that we wear in life." This simply means that all of us have the potential of doing everything in life that we REALLY WANT TO DO. The problem is, knowingly or unknowingly, WE PLACE LIMITATIONS AND BARRIERS ON OURSELVES. We blame others and situations for our lack of achievement and accomplishment but in the end, the blame must be put where it belongs . . . ON US.

The key to overcoming limitations and barriers is a strong, healthy attitude about yourself and your potential, a strong belief in yourself. It boils down to being able to turn the MINUSES into PLUSES, to make lemonade out of lemons, to produce desired results—not excuses and to be strong enough to ignore the "negatives" around you. CEILINGS ARE SELF-IMPOSED.

Inner strength makes successful people. Thomas Edison was probably one of the greatest inventors that ever lived. He harnessed electricity and put it to work. He gave the world light with his incandescent light bulb. He gave music with the phonograph. And he was able to do this despite that fact that he was almost totally deaf!

A reporter once asked him if his deafness wasn't a handicap. "On the contrary," he said, "deafness has been a great asset to me. It has saved me from a lot of useless chatter and it has taught me to hear from within."

Edison refused to put limitations and barriers on himself because of his deafness. He refused to allow frustrations, fears or regrets to get the better of him even though he met with 10,000 failures before he perfected the electric light. He never gave up. He simply continued to tap his inner resources and the power of his own mind.

I have found that successful people like Edison concentrate on future objectives. They do not dwell in the past, on defeats or disappointments. Rather than wait for others to show them the way, *they find their own way*. They rely on self-confidence, positive thinking and inner strength REFUSING TO PUT MENTAL BARRIERS ON THEMSELVES.

Charles Kettering broke his arm while cranking his car. Kettering was a master at turning minuses into pluses, lemons into lemonade, and immediately went to work on a new idea for starting cars that would be safer and better. In a short time he had invented the "self-starter."

GARBAGE IN—GARBAGE OUT

Program your computer for overcoming barriers. Father Dressel of Creighton Prep high school in Omaha is a genius at writing programs for computers. This man knows exactly what has to be done to get the maximum results from a computer. He has written two computer programs for my wife and me. His mind is absolutely "fabulous."

When we first got our computer, Father Dressel made a point of telling us "GARBAGE IN—GARBAGE OUT!" You get OUT of that computer EXACTLY what you PUT IN. If the program is as much as one little "character" or "letter" off the machine will not function properly. If you don't FEED IN material properly, an "ERROR" will immediately appear on the screen and the machine will not function properly. You GET OUT of that machine exactly what you PUT IN that machine.

Our minds are like that machine. Our minds will function exactly by the INPUT, garbage in—garbage out. *Positive thoughts in, positive results out; negative thoughts in, negative thoughts out.* By the results we obtain we can tell if an error has been made, if we are really alert and trying to get positive desired results and if we really have our heart set on accomplishing something good. You can't fool the computer and you can't fool your mind.

OPTIMISM IN—POSITIVE DESIRED RESULTS OUT

Pete Rose, who once was third baseman of the Cincinnati Reds, told a reporter, "Hitting a baseball is the hardest thing to do in all sports. Think about it: You've got a round ball and a round bat and the object is to hit it 'square.' No one can help you. There's nobody running interference and blocking for you." Pete Rose could have gone on to say that the situation is really even tougher than that. In fact, it's almost unfair because not only is the batter alone, he's competing against nine other guys . . . simultaneously!

All of that didn't stop Pete Rose from setting a record!! Rose's name has gone down in the record books as the player who has had a hit in the most consecutive games in baseball's National League.

Pete Rose has let many challenges drive him on to positive results and to set a new record, to break an old barrier. He programmed his mind for success and did exactly what the program called for . . . setting a record.

OPPORTUNITY VS CHANCES

The optimist looks at a new challenge and he feels like he is taking advantage of a real opportunity. The pessimist looks at the same challenge and feels like he is taking a real chance. A big difference!! A pessimist says, "I'll believe it when I see it." The optimist says, "I'll see it when I believe it!" An optimist looks at a half of a glass of water and says that it's half full. The pessimist looks at the same glass and says that it's half empty.

Henry Ford, the man who put America on wheels, finally decided in 1928 that he would abandon the T model and come out with the A model Ford. He produced a trial model and assigned the task of a thorough study of the new model to two of his engineers. The first engineer reported that the engine was too strong for the body; the horse-power must be reduced. The second engineer reported that the body was too weak for the engine; the body must be strengthened. It is unnecessary to tell you which engineer became the head of the engineering department of Ford Motor Company because he SAW THE OPPORTUNITY.

Two ships went out into the oyster bed areas. One crew soon returned stating that the oysters, which contained the pearls, were too deep for the diving gear. The other crew came back to port for new gear stating that the helmets were too weak for the depth they were required to go. I don't have to tell you which got "desired results."

Two men were sent out with hacksaws to salvage the bottom of a boat for scrap iron. One returned dejectedly and said the task was impossible; the iron was too hard for the saws. The other man came back and requested a saw of strongest steel saying that the saw was too weak. You know which man "made things happen."

We must make opportunities out of challenges every day. Every day is full of opportunities to the real "Pro," because every day is filled with new and exciting challenges.

LEARN TO SEE

Learn to see exactly what you really want. No fuzzy pictures. Get your camera (your mind) in perfect focus! Jim Bope, President of the Hop-Cap Company in Bremen, Indiana, is an example of what I'm talking about when I say "learn to see."

I had the pleasure of conducting a seminar for Jim and got acquainted with him. Jim told me he didn't have a formal education and for several years worked as a carpenter. Then he got an idea and he saw the thing he really wanted to do. Barriers didn't stand in his way. What he saw in his mind was put into action immediately.

His idea . . . to build truck covers, van conversions, mini motor homes and travel trailers. He has built a very successful company and is a real success. He's one of those select people who put ideas into action and did not let barriers stand in his way. His business slogan, "The company with imagination."

Ignore What Others Have Done—Go After The Things You Want. Roger Bannister is a young doctor in England. He'll probably never be remembered for his medical achievements, but almost every sports-minded person will recall how he got into the record books. As far as anyone knew, no athlete had been able to run

one mile in four minutes or less since men started to run races
and to compete for cherished prizes. Most people said it just
couldn't be done.

Roger Bannister didn't believe the experts. He began to plan
the way he would do it and he started to train and to work out
his plan. On May 6, 1954, HE ERASED THE MENTAL BARRIER
by running the first recorded four-minute mile. After this, amazing
things began to happen; another runner ran the mile in less than
four minutes, then another and then another. In a short period
of the next four years, the four-minute mile was run by about
forty-six runners. Roger Bannister had erased a mental barrier.
Its effect on other people proved what a valuable thing he had
given.

DON'T PUT LIMITATIONS ON YOURSELF

I have found that people sell themselves short and that they
have a tendency to CONFORM with the 95% that PLACE LIMI-
TATIONS on themselves and on their thinking.

Recently, I was asked by a man to set a worthy goal for
him. I refused because a goal has to be a personal thing and
we should not compare ourselves with other people. We should
set goals based on our own record as to what we have done
in the past and exactly what we want to do in the future.

Use the past as the foundation for setting your goals and
proceed from that point. You see, there's no way that I could
set a goal for that person. I might be putting SERIOUS LIMITA-
TIONS on his thinking if I didn't set the goal high enough, thus
putting MENTAL BARRIERS and LIMITATIONS on him. On
the other hand, I might have set a goal way too high and he
would have become FRUSTRATED.

Several years ago, I was inside the Colorado State Penitentiary waiting for the guard to open the door so that I could make my exit. (I did a lot of work in the Colorado Penitentiary with convicts helping to rehabilitate them.) The sheriff from Denver and his deputy arrived with four convicts who were sentenced to do time in the penitentiary.

I watched the sheriff and his assistant open up the back door of the station wagon and help these four men out of the car and up the stairs. They were bound with handcuffs and leg chains. It was a breathtaking and emotional experience to see these four men entering the walls where they would be confined. Those men, by their acts, really placed the chains of restraint upon themselves by their bad thinking and actions. They were now confined to the inside of the TALL WALLS which they could not hurdle over or escape.

The story is told about the farmer who placed a baby pumpkin inside of a mason fruit jar to see how large it would grow and the shape it would take. The pumpkin grew to fill the jar and could grow no more. The growth stopped with the size and shape of the jar. IT COULD NOT EXPAND. The LIMITATIONS had been placed on the pumpkin by the farmer.

I have often thought we do a similar thing with our minds by placing chains, limitations and high walls around us . . . limitations over which we cannot mentally jump.

The playwright, Archibald McLeash, said, "The only thing about a man that is a man is his mind, everything else can be found in a pig or in a horse." Realize right now that we place MENTAL BARRIERS in our minds ourselves and we cannot blame others or situations for our shortcomings.

Erase the negative mental barriers that we now have in our minds and replace those pictures with positive, successful, fulfilling images, realizing our minds are the only thing that can take us to our destination in life.

If you want to be a leader, you must create and visualize yourself doing *that* successfully. If you want to be a real professional, executive, salesperson, etc. you must create and visualize yourself doing *that* successfully.

STRETCH YOUR MIND

A biologist tells how he watched an ant carrying a piece of straw which seemed a big burden for it. The ant came to a crack in the earth which was too wide for it to cross. The ant stood for a time as though pondering over the situation. Then it put the straw across the crack and walked upon it.

Here is a lesson for every one of us. Our burdens can be made into a bridge for new progress. All progress of mankind has been made by people desiring to break records, to overcome burdens, to excel, and to meet challenges that have been thrown at them, to do things better and to do things that no one else has ever done. Talk about breaking mental barriers . . . just look at our "space program." A "you can't stop me" progressive attitude is the bridge and key to breaking mental barriers. Stretch your mind and see yourself doing better and bigger things.

HOW DO YOU SEE YOURSELF?

One afternoon my son, Greg, who was an honor student at Colorado Springs High School, was ready to quit physics. He said it was too difficult and he just didn't like the subject. I said, "How do you see yourself, Greg?" The reply was "flunking the course." We visited for a while and then he began to see that it was a very important subject for his future and that he could do as well at that as he did in his other subjects. He saw himself in a new light, the barriers were gone and he went from a "D" to an "A."

I have seen this same thing happen to many people. As soon as they erase the mental barriers—Zoom—they are on their way!

In the free enterprise system and the land of opportunity, no one places any restrictions on your productivity, what you want to be and what you want to do. *Erase the old negative mental barriers* and proceed full speed ahead and *become the successful person you really want to become* by creating new, exciting, positive mind pictures.

▲ ▲ ▲ ▲

"GARDLINES" *by Grant G. Gard*

DON'T TALK ABOUT THESE THINGS—DO THEM NOW!!

1. Analyze—How do I really see myself—What LIMITATIONS have I placed on myself?
2. ERASE all negative mental barriers and limitations on your thinking.
3. Replace restrictive thoughts and pictures with new POSITIVE END RESULT PICTURES.
4. Do not let other people place limitations on you.
5. Remove any handcuffs and chains you have placed on yourself and know that YOU CAN SET NEW RECORDS.
6. LIFT YOURSELF from "lows" to new "highs" by breaking old barriers.
7. STRETCH YOUR MIND DAILY to break old barriers.
8. Rely on your INNER STRENGTH and your ABILITIES.
9. Program your mind for ACHIEVEMENT . . . Garbage in—Garbage out.
10. Make opportunities out of challenges.

▲   ▲   ▲   ▲

Thought Provoking Quotes

"A vision without a task is a dream; A task without a vision is drudgery; A vision and a task is the hope of the world."

—Unknown

"The greatest discovery of my generation is that human beings can alter their lives by altering their attitudes of mind."

—William James

"The doors we open and close each day decide the lives we live."

—Flora Whittemore

"One may walk over the highest mountain—one step at a time."

—John Wanamaker

"Don't curse the darkness—light a candle."

—Chinese Proverb

"If you could kick the man responsible for most of your troubles, you wouldn't sit down for a week."

—Owen Arnold

"If you are resolutely determined to make a lawyer of yourself, the thing is more than half done already . . . Always bear in mind that your own resolution to succeed is more important than any one thing."

—Abraham Lincoln

"You better not compromise yourself—It's all you got."

—Jarvis Joplin

"It were not best that we should all think alike; it is difference of opinion that makes horse races."

—Mark Twain

"A man can succeed at almost anything for which he has unlimited enthusiasm."

—Charles Schwalb

"The important thing in life is to have great aim and to possess the aptitude and the perserverence to attain it."

—*Johann Wolfgang Von Goethe*

"Hell begins on the day when God grants us a clear vision of all that we might have achieved, of all the gifts which we have wasted, of all that we might have done which we did not do . . . For me the conception of Hell lies in two words—TOO LATE."

—*Gian-Carlo-Menotti*

"Omeletes are not made without breaking eggs."

—*Maximilien Francois*

"No one objects to a man being himself if he's trying to do better."

—*G. Norman Collie*

Never give up! If adversity presses,
Providence wisely has mingled the cup.
And the best counsel, in all your distresses,
Is the stout watchword of "Never give up!!"
—Martin F. Tupper

"When wealth is lost, nothing is lost.
When health is lost, something is lost.
When character is lost, all is lost."
—*Unknown*

11 | *The Grass is* Not *Always Greener*

Don't Overlook the Gold in Your Own Windows. Many years ago, a man and his wife lived in a small home on the east side of a very large lake. Each morning they would arise before the sun came up and they would begin work in their garden before the heat of the day. As they worked, they would look across the lake and they would see what appeared to be a castle on the other side. They knew it must be a castle because of the way the windows shone with a beautiful golden color.

One day the man said to his wife, "Today I'm going to take the boat and row all the way across the lake and go see that castle," and he began his journey across the water. It was noon before he arrived on the other side. He tied his boat to a shrub and made his way up the narrow path to the castle on the top of the hill. He found himself right in front of what he had thought to be a castle, but was surprised and disappointed to find it was a cottage even more humble than his own.

He went back down the path and began rowing back across the lake to tell his wife the news. He rowed several hours and found himself still out in the lake when the sun began to set. He looked up toward his home and was amazed to see that it was now the one with the golden windows. Then he realized that for all these years he had been living under an illusion.

This is so true with life—often we see a false picture when we look at other people and their accomplishments. WE OVER-LOOK THE GOLD IN OUR OWN WINDOWS—the precious little things that we have now and that we should not take for granted.

YOU TAKE YOUR PROBLEMS WITH YOU

I have found that many times people think the man or woman down the street has a "better deal," "better situation," or "better life." I do not want to BLOCK ANYONE'S PROGRESS if a change is in order, but many times when you move from one job to the next you find out two things; one, the new job wasn't as rosy as it appeared to be; and two, YOU TAKE YOUR "PROBLEMS" WITH YOU. You see, many people don't realize that it really ISN'T THE JOB or SITUATION when things don't go right. IT'S USUALLY THE PERSON and we take the same person right along with us unless we are really DEAD SET and DETERMINED on CHANGING something in our life. *When the grass looks greener on the other side of the fence, it may be that they are taking better care of it over there!!*

Dr. Stewart McClelan, President of Lincoln Memorial University in Illinois, told me . . . "When a man doesn't succeed at something he starts, he either didn't want to do it badly enough or else he convinced himself it couldn't be done."

You may be standing in your castle with golden windows

right now if you just don't give up wanting to do something badly enough and will do the things necessary to bring about your true success. The difference, many times, between success and failure is a very fine line.

I was watching a baseball game on TV and the right fielder ran back to the wall and made a terrific catch. The next time the ball was hit to him, he ran, jumped, but the ball went over his glove by about two inches . . . the runner made two bases. The difference between success and failure was only two inches.

My wife, Anita, is a really lovely gal who has many excellent qualities. One of the things she does so well is cook . . . it seems like everything she turns out in the kitchen has that little bit of extra good taste. When I ask her, "How do you make it taste so good?" She always replies, "I just add a little bit of this and a little bit of that."

She's a "Pro" . . . she knows that a little bit of this and a little bit more of something else makes for a successful end product. That "little bit" is what makes the difference between something being *mediocre* and something being *outstanding* or *superb*. I am convinced it's that "little bit extra" of attitude, desire and thinking that makes the difference between being *good* and being *first-rate.*

WE CREATE OUR OWN PROBLEMS

As I have stressed, we blame others for our circumstances and our shortcomings. REALIZE WE CREATE OUR OWN PROBLEMS!! We are, this very minute, what we have allowed and what we have made ourselves to be, nothing more or nothing less. In the end, there's only one person in this world you can cheat and that is yourself. So before you "give up," get depressed, or make a change, examine these three vital areas . . .

A + D + HR = ME

Ability—Have you developed your ability to do the thing you really want to do so that you are a real pro? Are you contributing or extracting? Are you further developing your abilities everyday to improve your effectiveness and to make yourself more valuable?

Desire—Do you really have a strong burning desire?

Human Relations—Have you developed your human relations skills and your "people know-how" to get desired results in working with people? Do you fully realize that regardless of your profession or occupation you are in the people business?

Those three things pretty well determine what you will be as a person, on and off the job.

Examine yourself closely and analyze yourself by the following examples:

Here's Example #1—

Ability and Desire, but no Human Relations. Here's a group of people . . . Smart, have a desire to do a good job, but plainly just don't know how to get along with people. They don't understand the importance of being able to work successfully with people. Many times they are not aware they have a serious problem. Many times they just don't want to be around and work with people.

It's this group that accounts for the fact that about 90% of the people who are fired from their jobs were discharged because they couldn't work smoothly with people.

A great amount of "job knowledge" is lost in this group because they cannot relate their "job knowledge" to people. Many people in this category lose out on pay raises, promotions, and commissions.

This type of person can be real creative with *things,* but not with *people.* This person really doesn't understand motivation and finds it hard to handle "human situations" as they arise and finds it very difficult to adjust to different "people situations." This type of person rarely, if ever, sees things from the other person's viewpoint and doesn't use "empathy" in dealing with people. This type rubs people the wrong way.

This type person doesn't realize this is a very competitive world and that *people* make the difference in meeting and beating competition. Good "HR's" give us the *competitive edge.*

Surveys have been run and they clearly show that as high as 68% of the people who refuse to do business with a particular store or work with a certain company refuse to do so because of a discourtesy, a personality conflict, or lack of good human relations with a representative of that company. This means lack of good "HR" cost companies many new and repeat customers and it also means lack of good internal HR causes a very expensive, high personnel turn-over.

The person who can get desired results through people is, by far, in the highest paid ranks today.

Here's Example #2—

Desire and Human Relations, But no Ability. This person is hindered badly. I'm certainly not implying this person is dumb or stupid, BUT I am saying that person is trying to do something that he or she isn't cut out to do or for which he or she isn't prepared. This type has not EARNED THE RIGHT to be doing the thing he or she is doing either through experience or study. They can learn a planned routine. They don't understand the potential of a person's mind, they don't do their homework, and they don't think for themselves. They do not want to be creative. They will do exactly what they are told to do AND NOT ANOTHER THING. This type person does not WIN THE CONFIDENCE of others and many times will have a POOR SELF-IMAGE. They get frustrated easily. Oh, this type will make a living but that's about all.

This type does not want to be bothered by going to seminars and workshops to improve abilities and learn how best to use those abilities. This type is pretty well satisfied where they are right now. They'll take more if given to them, but they won't pay the price to make themselves more valuable. They don't understand that you have to GIVE before you are going to RECEIVE. They fail to realize you must make yourself more valuable before the rewards are going to come.

To further develop your ABILITY, there are three types of goals to take into consideration:

Family goals

Business or Job goals

Improvement goals

Around 95% of the people would number those goals in importance like this:

1. Family goals

2. Business or Job goals

3. Improvement goals

This, obviously is wrong. They have the laws of life backwards because they are saying, "When I get this for my family and when my job is better to me, then I'm going to take time to improve MYSELF and my ABILITIES." Everything starts with the individual.

In setting these goals you should, of course, have them numbered like this:

1. Improvement goals

2. Business or Job goals

3. Family goals

The sad thing is this group has all kinds of potential, as we all do, but they just don't develop themselves further with the necessary KNOWLEDGE to IMPROVE THEIR ABILITY to handle their job as a "Pro." A Quality Performer, one who obtains complete knowledge, applies this knowledge to people and situations correctly and works wisely to obtain desired results.

Example #3—

Ability and Human Relations, but no Desire. Lots of people fall into this category. These people are smart, they have charm. They wish for more, but that's where it stops . . . they have no burning desire to really go after more. Fear is prevalent in this group. This type person is very content in his or her "COMFORT ZONE." They can do just about anything they want to do, but the problem is that THEY JUST PLAINLY DON'T WANT TO. They are FOLLOWERS, not leaders, very insecure, are not self-starters, and they do not have "happy discontentment." They are afraid to try anything new and are very satisfied with the "status quo."

This type person puts the people they are working for into early graves. This type person is practically impossible to motivate because he or she is very happy where he or she is.

Many of this type are the chronic complainers, the aginers, have a bad case of EXCUSITIS, and love to talk about all the reasons why new ideas won't work and why it can't be done.

Now—

Ability and Human Relations and Desire. The best example that I can think of is Abraham Lincoln. He worked hard to develop his abilities and human relations skills. I studied Abraham Lincoln and I think he was one of the greatest men who ever lived. He should be a real inspiration to all of us because he started with only one thing and that was DESIRE and developed himself from that point on.

Check your situation and see where your strengths and weaknesses are. See where the problem really is . . . that is, if you feel you have one. The pasture may be or may not be greener on the other side of the fence. It might be, if you change your situation, that you'll take the same problems with you. You'll take the good positive qualities with you, too!!

This is why it's important to DO THE RIGHT THINGS RIGHT at an early age so that you can establish a good "track" or "record." *A person has a tendency to do in the future what he has done in the past.* We keep repeating . . . in a cycle. This is why companies always measure a person by his past record and performance . . . the desired results he has been able to obtain.

I know a highly successful manager of a leading company in Colorado Springs. He was chosen for the manager's job of a different company because of his past track. He accepted because he wanted the challenge to make this company grow, plus it was an even better opportunity for him. He is doing very well and so is the company he is managing. He took all of his skills and result-oriented abilities with him to the new job. What he did once he is doing again and he will continue to do.

THE TOUCHSTONE

It was said that when the great Library of Alexandria burned that everything was destroyed but one book. It wasn't a valuable book. As a matter of fact, it was sold to a poor man for just a few coppers. The man who bought it couldn't read much, but inside he found a strip of vellum that told the secret of the Touchstone.

The Touchstone was a small warm pebble, a black pebble that was lost someplace on the shores of the Black Sea. It was said that anyone who owned the Touchstone would have the power to turn ordinary metal into precious gold. So he sold his few belongings—he bought a few simple supplies and went to the Black Sea. He pitched his tent near the sea and started searching for the Touchstone.

His instructions said that the Touchstone would be warm to the touch. He picked up a pebble, it was cold, so he threw it into the sea. He picked up another pebble, it was cold so he threw it into the sea. He went on searching for many days for the warm, black pebble. Finally months passed and then a year— then two years and finally, he had searched for three years. And all this time he had been picking up pebbles and throwing them into the sea because they were cold.

Then one morning he picked up the warm, black pebble, but he threw IT into the sea because he had formed the habit. Our lives are governed by the habits we form. One noted philosopher said, "Cultivate only the habits you are willing should master you."

Many times we are acting and talking certain ways because "habit" has control of us, good or bad. We are all creatures of habit, but we must be strong enough to analyze ourselves and discard negative working and living habits. Create and visualize in your mind yourself as a strong person using only good positive habits.

Look for the gold in your own windows and develop your A + D + HR to the fullest.

▲   ▲   ▲   ▲

"GARDLINES" *by Grant G. Gard*

DON'T TALK ABOUT THESE THINGS—DO THEM NOW!!

1. Take a good LOOK at your job—does it really hold you back or is the pasture truly greener on the other side of the fence?
2. Handle your career in such a way that you USE THE GOLD AROUND YOUR WINDOWS.
3. Do you fully understand the phrase "WE CREATE OUR OWN PROBLEMS?"

4. Don't take the same old problems with you. If you change situations, CORRECT ALL PROBLEM AREAS.
5. Analyze the pasture on the other side of the fence—what does it have to offer that you cannot obtain now with the right A + D + HR?
6. If you have outgrown your present opportunity, WHEN DO YOU PLAN TO DO SOMETHING ABOUT IT?
7. Be determined to develop only GOOD WORKING and LIVING HABITS.
8. Develop your A + D + HR to the fullest.

▲ ▲ ▲ ▲

THOUGHT PROVOKING QUOTES

"The talent for success is nothing more than doing what you can do well and doing well whatever you do."

—Longfellow

"Success does not consist in never making mistakes but in never making the same one a second time."

—George Bernard Shaw

"We often discover what will succeed by finding out what will not. Probably he who never made a mistake never made a discovery."

—Anonymous

"It is in men as in soils where sometimes there is a vein of gold which the owner knows not of."

—Swift

"Action may not always bring happiness—but there is no happiness without action."

—Disraeli

"Strong beliefs win strong men, and then make them stronger."

—Walter Bagehot

"Life is too short to be little."

—Disraeli

"Every noble work is at first impossible."
  —*Thomas Carlyle*

"I never allow myself to become discouraged under any circumstances. The three great essentials to achieve anything worthwhile are first, hard work; second, stick-toitivness; third, common sense."
  —*Thomas A. Edison*

"The mind is its own place and in itself can make a heaven of Hell; a hell of Heaven."
  —*John Milton*

"They can conquer who believe they can . . . He has not learned the first lesson of life who does not every day surmount a fear."
  —*Ralph Waldo Emerson*

"Nothing great was ever achieved without enthusiasm."
  —*Emerson*

"Shallow men believe in luck."
  —*Persian Proverb*

"Fear isn't cowardice. Cowardice is failure to fight fear. The weakling feels fear and quits. The man of courage feels fear and fights."
  —*Arnold H. Glasow*

"It is better to have a right destroyed than to abandon it because of fear."
  —*Phillip Mann*

12 | *The Art of Speaking to One or Many*

HOW TO COMMUNICATE EFFECTIVELY—ONE TO ONE

People are not persuaded by what we say, only by what they understand and feel. Be careful what you say and how you say it . . . someone may be taking you literally.

The green carpet in the oval office of the White House during the Truman administration was treadbare and pretty well worn out.

Mr. Truman very casually made this observation to one of his White House aides saying, "It would be nice to have a new rug in here." Nothing more was said at the time.

A few weeks later, Truman left the White House for a short vacation in Independence, Missouri, his hometown. Upon his return, he was pleasantly surprised to see a plush new carpet, complete with the presidential seal sewn in, on the floor of his oval office.

175

He wasn't so pleased a few days later when he discovered the invoice amounting to several hundred dollars for a new oval office rug. Mr. Truman personally approved invoices for White House expenses.

He immediately demanded of his aides the name of the person responsible for ordering such an expensive rug. "You did, sir," came the reply.

"I didn't order the rug," Truman said. "All I said was that it would be nice to have a new one" . . . to which the aide replied, "Sir, when the President says he would like something, it means to an aide—go get it."

THE 5 APPRAISAL AREAS OF COMMUNICATION

One of the most important elements of success is to be able to communicate our ideas effectively to others. An IDEA, SERVICE or CONCEPT is NO BETTER than the way we can COMMUNICATE with other people. We want to communicate so that others can see clearly in their minds the thing that we are talking about . . . we learn by pictures so we have to describe the thing we want to communicate, so that accurate mental images are formed. We also communicate our feelings. We want others to feel as we feel. Here are five ways we communicate—

1. What we say
2. How we say it
3. What we do (actions)
4. How we do it
5. How we look

We must communicate so that there can be no MISUNDERSTANDING and that everyone gets the same meaning and feeling from what we are saying.

A professor in a hygiene class at a college was preparing his lesson on the harmful effects of whiskey. He placed two glasses on his desk, one filled with whiskey and the other one filled with water. He took his tongs and picked up an earthworm and placed it in the glass of water and said, "Now, students, you can see that the worm is swimming and alive in the water." He then placed the worm in the whiskey and it immediately curled up and died. The professor said, "Now you can see the harmful effects of whiskey. The earthworm lived in the water, but curled up and died immediately in the whiskey. So never drink whiskey."

Some guy in the back of the classroom got up and said, "You got it all wrong, Prof. Proves to me that if you drink whiskey you won't have worms."

The point is that people interpret differently the things that we say, so we have to make sure we are communicating clearly and have everyone understanding what we are saying.

A school teacher I had in my high school in Overton, Nebraska, was a very brilliant person, but she had one big problem. She couldn't get her point across. She gave a math test one day, flunked 90% of the class and thought all of the students were dumb. No one understood what she was trying to get across and the test showed it. Her feed-back should have been to sharpen her communicative skills. But, no, she did like others do so many times . . . *she blamed the people on the receiving end rather than on the sending end.* There's a favorite expression of mine that I love and have made it part of my nervous system—"IF IT'S FUZZY IN THE PULPIT, IT'S REAL CLOUDY IN THE PEW."

SPECIFICITY VS. GENERALITY

First you have to know exactly what you want to say. You must get a mind picture of the thing you are talking about and practice describing it until you are certain that the other person will clearly understand everything you have said. Be specific . . . never general . . .

State	Don't State
A box 4 feet by 2 feet	It was a large box
5000 people attended	A lot of people attended
3 month-old baby	A new baby

Ask frequently, have I made myself clear?

Secondly, remember we communicate not only in words, but also by actions and feelings. Be SINCERE when communicating, LISTEN ATTENTIVELY and take great interest in what the other person is saying, so that you can communicate with true sincerity.

Thirdly, be EXCITED IN YOUR COMMUNICATION. Keep people awake!! MAKE THE OTHER PERSON FEEL AS YOU FEEL. We transfer our feelings and emotions, as I have said before, and part of good communication is making the other person feel as you do. We can't give something away we do not have, so we have to live in a world of excitement if we are going to give others this feeling.

Fourthly, KEEP IT SIMPLE . . . Yes, talk in language that everyone can understand. I know of people who try to impress others with their big words. I know you have probably heard of the KISS formula: K-keep; I-it; S-simple; S-stupid. There's a great deal of truth and advice in that old formula.

Good communication helps us to make favorable first impressions as well as to get our point across with real meaning. *You and I have heard first-rate ideas expressed poorly outstripped by second-rate ideas expressed well.*

GOOD COMMUNICATION MEANS FAVORABLE RECOGNITION

By expressing your ideas well and communicating effectively, you will get favorable recognition. For the practice of putting instructions into words, try telling your wife how to smoke a cigarette. You and your wife are from Mars and have never seen a cigarette. Tell her specifically how to smoke one, starting with a new package that has never been opened. Try telling someone how to put on a jacket.

BE BRIEF AND TO THE POINT

BE BRIEF . . . get to the point quickly. I know of people who take all day to say what a good, sharp communicating person could say in 20 minutes. The only way this person can say less and less is to talk more and more.

BE BRIEF and SPECIFIC . . . RIGHT TO THE POINT. We can turn people off if we talk too much. It's happened to me and it could happen to you. People do not like to hear someone ramble on and on. In fact, I was in the office of a company president one day when a salesman was explaining his product and service and finally the president said, "You have been here 15 minutes and have said nothing. What is it that you are trying to tell me?" The salesman lost a large sale. You don't have time to waste and neither does anyone else.

BE YOURSELF

BE YOURSELF . . . LET YOUR PERSONALITY HELP YOU TO COMMUNICATE. Yes, don't try to be anyone except yourself. Know a lot more about your idea, service, concept or product than you can use. Be prepared and armed with the facts. It will help you to communicate with CONFIDENCE and let your PERSONALITY SHINE. Remember, YOUR PERSONALITY IS YOU . . . it better be. Be yourself! Be confident! All of these things help you communicate your ideas effectively.

VITAL AREAS TO CONSIDER

Several areas you should seriously think about and be very much aware of for effective communication to really enable you to get your point across are:

ASSUMPTIONS

You assume certain things and the other person assumes certain things. You should try to find out what assumptions the other person has so that you can communicate without misunderstanding. If you are both assuming the same thing, there will be communication. However, if your assumptions are not the same, there will never be effective communication. Never leave a person assuming something that is not correct.

VIEWPOINTS

Everyone has viewpoints about their job, company, product, profession, problems that they want solved and about you. Try to figure out the other person's viewpoint and to see things from that person's point of view. Communicate from that person's viewpoint. However, you may have to change some of that person's views in order for that person to see the true picture. This will take tact and diplomacy . . . and that is the mark of a real Pro.

FEELINGS

You have certain feelings and the other person has certain feelings. The other person may feel all bad or all good about you. Ask yourself "Why does the other person feel the way he or she does and what causes that person to act or react this way?"

Try to understand those feelings so that you can talk that person's language and come up with mutual feelings.

ATTITUDE

Every person has an attitude about anything and everything. Try to figure out that attitude. Is it for you or is it against you? Warm? Cold? What has made that person have that attitude? What can you say in communication to help that person have a different attitude that would be better? Changing a person's attitude is a real challenge. Be careful how you express yourself here.

Also, it is very important to take a PERSON'S TEMPERA-MENT into consideration for effective communication:

Choleric. The choleric individual is intense, very strong-minded and strong-willed. That individual is going to go through life intent on achieving worthy goals despite all obstacles. This type of person will do just about anything to get what he or she wants.

Phlegmatic. This type of individual is the exact opposite of the choleric. This type is quiet and unassuming, seldom gets worked up or real exicted. This type is very intelligent, but the approach to life is entirely different. This type of person will accomplish as much as the choleric type, but will do it in a quiet manner.

Sanguine. The sanguine type of person sees the world through rose-colored glasses. This type is cheerful; the eternal optimist; and sees only the good things in life and has a rosy outlook about everything.

Melancholic. The melancholic type of person is the very negative-minded person. He or she sees things from the dark side of life, never getting close to people or on friendly terms with them. This type prefers to be a loner, off in the corner, continually painting a "black picture" as to how bad things are.

Each person's temperament is a combination of these four basic temperaments. However, one of these four temperaments will be dominant.

To really be successful and effective in communicating with people, we must understand their assumptions, viewpoints, feelings and attitudes and take into consideration the four temperaments of an individual: Choleric; Phlegmatic; Sanguine; and Melancholic, as well as all of the other previously mentioned important points.

HOW TO SPEAK TO GROUPS . . . COMFORTABLY

Many times I have been asked the question, "Is there really a way to develop poise and self-confidence when I am called upon to speak to a group?" Frequently I hear these words, "When I am called upon to stand up and speak at a company meeting, a sales meeting, church group, civic group, etc., I just simply freeze. I am so self-conscious I cannot think clearly . . . I go blank. Is there anything a person can do to overcome this dreaded fear?" The answer to these questions is YES.

Twenty-five years ago I had this same feeling and was plagued with the same symptoms. I hated to get up in front of people, but I found out that by following certain ideas and techniques, by staying in there and never giving up and having the winning attitude, I could and did get to the point where it was pure enjoyment to speak to groups. I LOVE IT! The larger the audience the better. YOU CAN LEARN TO DO THE SAME THING.

First, review the preceeding pages carefully because many of the ideas and techniques that apply to individual communication will be effective in front of groups.

Second, sell yourself on the importance of whipping this fear. Think what it would mean to you in terms of peace, happiness, added success and inner enjoyment, because as we lose our fear of people we see ourselves in an entirely different light. As we gain even more self-confidence that same additional confidence carries right over to our profession and everyday life.

Any person can develop his or her own latent abilities if that person has sufficient desire to do so. Do not think that you are unusual and that your case is extremely difficult.

The first time Mark Twain stood up to speak in public he admitted that his mouth felt like it was filled with cotton and his pulse was speeding excessively. Lloyd George said that he was in a state of misery the first few times he attempted to speak in public. Even Lincoln felt shy for a few opening minutes of his speeches. So you have no fear that cannot be overcome. Do the thing you fear to do and the death of fear is certain.

In a nutshell, here are the techniques that will help you do a first-rate job speaking to groups:

1. DECIDE YOUR EXACT PURPOSE. Every speech has one of four purposes. You must know if your purpose is to convince, inform, entertain or motivate people into action.

2. EARN THE RIGHT. This means you must know your subject thoroughly, so that you become the authority and are worth listening to. You earn the right to speak on your subject by two ways: Through Study and By Experience.

3. BE EAGER. You must have a deep down conviction that you have a real message or point to get across. You must be eager to share your message with your group. If you have no particular desire to be speaking to the group, they will sense this and you will fail because you will be insincere.

4. BE ENTHUSIASTIC. The audience can never turn their backs on an enthusiastic speaker. The live wire in the

front of the room will capture and hold the attention of the group. If you are dull, dead, colorless as a speaker . . . do your audience a favor and stay home. The enthusiastic speaker radiates a positive attitude, radiates success and is magnetic.

5. NEVER, NEVER MEMORIZE. If you memorize your talk, you will find yourself using "canned" written language and if you happen to forget, you are in serious trouble and in an embarrassing situation. If you have ever "gone blank" before an audience, you know it's a horrible experience.

6. MAKE BRIEF NOTES. Three by five cards work very well for making your notes and are easily handled while you are in front of a group. Do not play with the note cards while speaking . . . this distracts. Have the note cards in order and well organized. Make every move look professional. Note cards will also let you concentrate on your message and you will not have to be concerned about overlooking some important point.

7. KNOW THOROUGHLY HOW YOU WILL OPEN YOUR TALK. Get the first 5 or 6 sentences well in mind as you must win the attention and the confidence of the listeners immediately. An impression is made within one minute after you start speaking so that means PLAN A STRONG, CAPTIVATING OPENER. Open your talk with a humorous example, a quote . . . something that arouses curiousity like a startling statement or ask a question and get a show of hands.

8. DON'T APOLOGIZE. Don't fall into the trap of telling the audience that you didn't have time to prepare. If you aren't prepared, the audience will certainly know this . . . you won't have to tell them. If you haven't been given

time to properly prepare, you should never have accepted the invitation to speak. You owe it to your audience to be well prepared. You are taking up their precious time. Lack of good preparation clearly shows lack of respect for the group.

9. ORGANIZE YOUR MATERIAL. Your material should be organized in a LOGICAL SEQUENCE and should be presented in such a way that you capture and hold the attention of the listeners.

10. EMPHASIZE IMPORTANT POINTS. This can be done by using many illustrations and examples. Illustrations and examples will make your points clearer and more vivid in the minds of the listeners. It will also enable the listeners to retain your message much longer. Use analogies. Restate important points.

11. USE DEMONSTRATIONS AND EXHIBITS. This helps you to be even more memorable since seeing a thing just once is worth a thousand words of description. Demonstrations and exhibits are also very helpful to the speaker since they help to get your mind off of yourself by drawing attention to the exhibit. A word of caution. . . . *Talk to the audience and not to the exhibit. Be sure that the demonstration and the exhibit can be seen by everyone in the audience.*

12. HAVE A PLEASANT EXPRESSION. An audience enjoys listening to a speaker who is having a good time presenting the talk. How can we expect the audience to enjoy *us* if we aren't enjoying ourselves?

13. SEE YOURSELF SUCCEEDING. Act as if it were impossible to fail. WE BECOME WHAT WE THINK ABOUT. If you believe that you will succeed, you will certainly succeed. I know you will have some fear when

you first begin, but very quickly you will have that fearful feeling under control.

14. GESTURES. Canned gestures get the same results as canned language. They are artificial. Be natural and THE GESTURING WILL TAKE CARE OF ITSELF. Watch a group of children playing. They gesture beautifully because they are expressing themselves naturally and they are involved. I'm saying . . . get involved with your speech and let the gestures flow naturally without worrying about them. If you are natural and involved, gestures will take care of themselves.

15. BE SPECIFIC. Don't use general terms. Use specific terms. Use terms that can leave no doubt and misunderstanding in the listeners' minds.

16. BE BRIEF. Don't bore the audience with excessive and meaningless details. Keep It Simple.

17. DRESS APPROPRIATELY. The spotlight is on you and you have only one chance to make a good impression. Good clothes also help to build confidence in the speaker and help you to build a good image.

18. HUMOR. If you can use humorous stories to get a good response from the audience, use them. However, if you are one of those persons who does not put humor over well, don't use humorous stories. We all have seen the speaker try to be funny and not get any response from the audience at all. In fact, in some cases, I have seen the audience actually feel sorry for the speaker. A speaker who is trying to be funny and cannot embarrasses everyone. My cardinal rule: Practice a humorous story 25 times before you try it in front of an audience. Get the timing down to perfection.

19. PAY SINCERE COMPLIMENTS. Audiences always

welcome sincere compliments. So find something that you can honestly and sincerely compliment them for.

20. STAY WITHIN YOUR TIME LIMIT. Don't exceed the time scheduled for your talk.

21. USE EASY CONVERSATIONAL LANGUAGE. Talk to the group as if you were talking to one person. What is a group? It is just individuals.

22. COMMUNICATE WITH YOUR LISTENERS. Avoid staring at the ceiling or the floor. Communicate with the listeners. Have the audience as close to you and as compact as possible. It is difficult to motivate a group that is scattered all over a room that is too large for the size of the group.

23. LEAVE THE AUDIENCE WANTING MORE. Always make it a point to stop talking while the audience is very receptive and wanting more. If you do this, you won't have people becoming bored and walking out on you.

24. BE YOURSELF. Don't try to be someone or something you are not.

25. HAVE A STRONG CLOSE. The close should be the climax of your talk and you should know thoroughly how you are going to wrap it up. The close, if memorable, will stay in the minds of the listeners the longest because it is the last thing to be remembered. You can close your talk by summarizing the important points you have made; using a poem; appealing for action; or you can close by leaving them laughing.

26. SPEAK LOUDLY ENOUGH SO THAT ALL CAN HEAR YOU. There isn't anything more disturbing to an audience than not being able to hear the speaker clearly. If you are using a microphone, arrive early and make sure it works properly.

27. MENTION THE NAMES OF SOME PERSONS IN THE AUDIENCE. This helps you to build a rapport with your group and makes your talk more personal.
28. PLAY YOURSELF DOWN AND NOT UP. Audiences love the speaker who doesn't brag about how great he or she is. They love the person who admits to making some mistakes or who tells a joke about himself. Of course, don't play yourself down to the point that the audience does not respect you and loses confidence in you.
29. BE A COLORFUL SPEAKER. Don't talk in a monotone. Change your pitch . . . louder, softer; emphasize certain words; pause effectively; vary your rate of speaking. Use enough variety to keep your speech interesting.
30. PRACTICE. Look for opportunities to give talks to service clubs, church groups, school groups, company meetings, etc., because NOTHING REPLACES PRACTICE. Practice and more practice will help you to wear away fear. You can read all kinds of books on public speaking, but they are meaningless until you are actually standing before a group and practicing the skills necessary for you to feel comfortable.

Here are some guidelines that you may want to consider following while you are preparing and organizing your material in a logical sequence.

1. SECURE INTERESTED ATTENTION.
2. WIN THE CONFIDENCE OF THE AUDIENCE.
3. STATE YOUR FACTS. EDUCATE THE AUDIENCE REGARDING THE MERITS OF YOUR PROPOSITION.
4. APPEAL TO THE MOTIVES THAT MAKE PEOPLE ACT; SUMMARIZE YOUR HIGH POINTS MAKING SURE EVERYONE IS INFORMED AND CONVINCED; CLOSE WITH A LIGHT JOKE THAT HAS A MESSAGE BEHIND IT TO LEAVE THEM LAUGHING.

or
1. STATE YOUR FACTS.
2. ARGUE FOR THEM.
3. APPEAL FOR ACTION.

or
1. SHOW THAT SOMETHING IS WRONG.
2. SHOW HOW TO REMEDY IT.
3. ASK FOR COOPERATION.

Yes, you can certainly develop your ability to speak to groups comfortably and effectively. It's all up to you and how determined you are. Never do anything thinking defeat. *Always make conditions right for success* and that means see yourself doing this very thing successfully and in a positive way; doing the things as outlined to attain achievement.

Keep practicing. Nothing will replace practice and experience. Practice and experience build "Confidence" and a "Winner." You will gain lots of favorable recognition for yourself, have a great amount of inner satisfaction and increase your effectiveness in getting "desired results" with people.

You can do anything you really want to do IF you want to do it badly enough.

▲   ▲   ▲   ▲

"GARDLINES" *by Grant G. Gard*

DON'T TALK ABOUT THESE THINGS—DO THEM NOW!

1. Be determined to sharpen all 5 areas, so that you will make a GOOD FIRST IMPRESSION:
> 1. What we say
> 2. How we say it
> 3. What we do
> 4. How we do it
> 5. How we look

2. Be determined to communicate so there can be NO MISUNDER-STANDING.
3. Make sure you are BRIEF, CLEAR AND SPECIFIC in communicating your ideas.
4. BE EAGER to communicate your ideas.
5. Put more true EXCITEMENT in your communication. It will help you communicate more effectively.
6. Keep it SIMPLE so everyone can understand.
7. Know exactly what you want to say. BE PREPARED.
8. UNDERSTAND the personality "make-up" of people.
9. PRACTICE the 30 Principles to become effective in front of groups. Practice will wear away fear and make you comfortable.

THOUGHT PROVOKING QUOTES

"Let thy speech be short, comprehending much in few words."
—Shakespeare

"A man is never master of an idea until he can express it clearly."
—Lew Sarett

"Everything that can be thought can be thought clearly."
—Ludwig Wittgenstein

"The man who graduates today and stops learning tomorrow is uneducated the day after."
—Newton D. Baker

"Leadership gravitates to the man who can talk."
—Lowell Thomas

"Use what language you will, you can never say anything but what you are."
—Emerson

"You must have a pleasant manner and be able to make a favorable impression within thirty seconds."
—Arthur C. Fuller

"Give me heart touch with all that live and strength to speak my word. But if that is denied me, give the strength to live unheard."

—Edwin Markham

"The ability to speak effectively is an acquirement rather than a gift."

—William Jennings Bryan

"Never allow yourself to go physically asleep if you expect to keep yourself mentally awake."

—Nathan Sheppard

"It is never safe to look into the future with eyes of fear."

—Edward Henry Harriman

"I have found that if I have faith in myself and in the idea I am tinkering with, I usually win out."

—Charles F. Kettering

"I never did anything worth doing by accident, nor did any of my inventions come by accident."

—Thomas A. Edison

"Patience and fortitude conquer all things."

—Ralph Waldo Emerson

"Enjoy your own life without comparing it with that of another."

—Condorcet

13 | *Effective Decision Making and Problem Solving*

"A problem," said Henry Kaiser, "is only opportunity in work clothes." People who face their problems, who try hard to solve them and make decisions, will seldom fail. Often they will reap benefits and rewards they had no way of foreseeing.

Years ago two brothers, Thaddeus and Erastus Fairbanks, were running a small hemp business. Their biggest difficulty was in trying to weigh this hemp with the crude and inaccurate scales of the day.

There had to be a better way and Thaddeus set about to find a better way. Eventually he devised a platform scale which solved their problem. Now they were able to weigh their hemp with some semblance of accuracy.

What happened then came as a complete surprise to the brothers. Many of their customers wanted to buy their scales . . . more than wanted to buy their hemp. So as a favor to these customers the two men made more scales. Soon the demand for their scales became so great that the brothers gave up the hemp business.

The success of their new enterprise led the Fairbanks brothers to a fortune they never dreamed of—all because they had THE COURAGE TO FACE A SIMPLE PROBLEM, THE IMAGINATION TO FIND A SOLUTION, and THE DETERMINATION TO ACT ON THEIR DECISION WITHOUT HESITATION.

Procrastination . . . the Graveyard Full of Good Ideas. How many times have you heard people say, "I can't make up my mind." "I'm afraid to try it." "Joe can do it, but I simply can't seem to get the job done." "It scares me to think of doing it." "What's the use, it won't turn out right anyway, so let's leave it as it is." "I know what I should do, but I just can't get sold on it."?

I could go on and on listing alibis for not making decisions. Procrastination is a graveyard full of good ideas or, to put it another way, PROCRASTINATION IS UNHAPPINESS. We cannot be "DOERS" and allow indecision to rule us. We cannot be productive and happy and let procrastination dominate us . . . nor can we grow in our jobs and increase our production because we are wasting time, wasting thinking ability and wasting useful resources on a quality that can help us do only one thing and this is "LOSE."

MAKE "DECISION MAKING" A HABIT

We are all creatures of habit and, if we habitually procrastinate, we should remind ourselves of the tremendous price we are paying for this negative habit. Procrastination is a fault that most people put off trying to correct.

PROCRASTINATION IS A LUXURY AND VERY FEW OF US CAN AFFORD IT! If we have decided not to decide on a problem, we ACTUALLY have made a decision. We made a decision NOT to make a decision and again we are off in the same old thought and habit pattern.

Write down on a piece of paper all of the reasons you can think of to be a DOER, A DECISION MAKER . . . then write down the ideas you have that favor INDECISION. Look back and see exactly what procrastination has been doing to your progress, your goal achievement and the many good things you want to do with your life. This idea should cause you NEVER TO PROCRASTINATE AGAIN. The price is too high to pay. Start today, right now, to say: "I WILL make every decision necessary for me to achieve my goals and I WILL make a habit of making DECISIONS ON TIME and as WISELY as possible."

I have heard it said that the best decisions made by high executives are decisions made QUICKLY after they obtain ALL the information necessary to make a decision. They are slow to change that decision once it has been made. The non-doers and "indecisive types" are slow to make a decision, if they ever make one, and fast to change it.

DECIDE WHAT YOU WANT

I know of people in their 50's and 60's who don't really know what they want from life. I have talked to many people who have been trying to decide "something" for themselves for months and even years . . . they still haven't gotten around to doing it! If you don't know what you want to do, how does anyone else know what you want to do? How can you hit a "target" if you haven't put a "target" up?

I visited with a 70-year-old dentist who told me that all of his life he wanted to take an active part in service clubs and church work in his little community and never had the COURAGE to make the DECISION to do so until he retired. Think of what that man has missed out on all through his life! Think, also, of the valuable ideas he could have contributed to the community had he made the decision to go ahead and do it many years ago!

It takes COURAGE to make decisions, but there is an old adage that says, "Once you've made up your mind to do a thing, it will be done." How true . . . the hard part is having the courage, overcoming the "ifs" and "reservations," the "self-doubt" and the "fear" that creeps in.

CREATE AND VISUALIZE in your mind the picture of the decisive-type person you really want to be. Block out all the negative, sidestepping, vacillating and detour pictures. Your positive mind picture will attract everything necessary for you to become exactly what you have decided to become. Likes attract likes. It may take some time, but keep the positive mind pictures in front of you at all times and continually sell yourself on the many advantages you now have over the person who doesn't make things happen because he cannot decide.

GET THE RIGHT INFORMATION

In making decisions, obtain information and ONLY THE BEST INFORMATION AVAILABLE to help you decide on solving problems. Write down the reasons FOR on one side of the paper and on the other side, write down the ideas OPPOSED. This will help you to see exactly what the right decision is for you. Get this information in a very impartial way, because we have a tendency to let into our minds only the information that agrees with our thinking. Remember—a decision is no better than the INFORMATION we use in making the decision. Set TIME LIMITS on when you will come up with this valuable information. Don't do "SURFACE THINKING" . . . do "IN DEPTH THINKING." This means extra work and effort, but it will be well worth it.

A prisoner at the Colorado State Penitentiary gave me a painting he had made in his cell as a token of appreciation for my working with the men. It was a picture of a cat. I took it home to my daughter, Kristie, and she didn't like it at all because it looked so sad, sitting in the corner of a room, tears coming down its face—very sad.

One day, a few months later, I came home from work and Kristie was all excited. She all at once had decided that she loved that picture. The picture hadn't changed. It was still that same old, sad cat. She said, "Dad, that isn't a picture of a sad cat, it's a picture of a man in prison who is sad." In the background were the concrete blocks like they use for some cells. Everything changed when Kris realized, in depth, the true meaning of the picture. The picture was a man expressing his own feelings and emotions.

Look IN DEPTH for causes to problems, don't just do surface thinking. When we go to a doctor with a headache, he tries, in depth, to find the true cause of the problem. He doesn't treat surface symptoms without finding out what the cause is. You'll be surprised how differently problems and decisions will become when you handle them with "IN DEPTH" thinking.

Again I caution you to throw out the old mind pictures, old thought patterns, old procrastination habits and only let in the new information which will help you to create and visualize the new mind picture of being that decisive person you really want to be. An "upset mind" means an "upset person." Stay calm and confident in building your mind pictures. SEE YOURSELF GOING THROUGH PROBLEMS and NOT RUNNING AROUND PROBLEMS.

ACTION—THE KEY

As my good friend Ken Lewis of General Motors would say—*"IF IT'S GOING TO BE—IT'S UP TO ME!!"* No one else can put you into ACTION but yourself, and your mind can decide. You can see good, successful mind pictures, but you still have to put yourself into action CARRYING OUT ALL OF THE THOUGHTS AND DECISIONS. It's all up to you.

FACE REALITY, THE CHALLENGES AND GO STRAIGHT AHEAD. Lots of people think knowledge is power—that's wrong. ACTION OF KNOWLEDGE IS POWER. Knowledge, wisdom, good thinking, positive mind pictures are all wasted unless you blast them into ACTION.

You'll be surprised how the positive thoughts and actions will attract more positive thoughts and actions. You've now got the ball rolling for yourself and it's starting to "mushroom." SUCCESS BREEDS MORE SUCCESS. Good decision-making habits breed more good decision-making habits.

WAITING GETS NOWHERE

I know a president of a bank in Colorado who told me, on several occasions, that he would much rather make a wrong decision and do something about it than make no decision at all. He is a very successful businessman. He said, "I can usually tell if a decision is wrong or not before it hurts too much and, from this experience, I can have the wisdom to make the right one. If I don't make any decision, I get absolutely nowhere."

LOOK FOR THE SIMPLEST SOLUTION TO SOLVE PROBLEMS

Harry Houdini was one of the world's greatest magicians. He charmed audiences with his great work. He was born in Wisconsin back in 1874, and spent much of his youth working in a local locksmith shop. It is said that there wasn't a knot he couldn't untie, there wasn't a lock he couldn't open.

He would often entertain his audiences by having his hands secured with handcuffs, having himself sealed in a box and then lowered into water. Within a few minutes he would free himself and float to the surface. He would go around the country allowing himself to be locked in cells of the strongest jails. The jailer was always bewildered when Houdini would set himself free within a very few minutes.

One time something went wrong. He went to a small town and straight to the jailer and challenged him to secure him in a cell. The jailer put him in handcuffs, a strait jacket and even chained his legs and then he left him in a locked cell.

In just a few moments, Houdini had freed himself of the handcuffs, the strait jacket and even the shackles on his legs. Then he went to work on the cell door. He worked for an hour, two hours and finally, in complete exhaustion, he leaned against the cell door and the door swung open. The jailer laughed and said, "Harry, I didn't bother to lock the cell door because I knew the lock wouldn't hold you anyway."

Well, Harry forgot to look for the SIMPLE SOLUTION. Isn't it that way with many of us? We are often inclined to look for a DIFFICULT SOLUTION to work out problems.

Our goal should always be—*that which is the simplest solution to bring us adequate results.*

5 STEPS TO EFFECTIVE DECISION MAKING AND PROBLEM SOLVING

Your progress in your career will depend on the quality of your decisions, the way you handle problems and the way you translate decisions into action.

There is something about making decisions that opens up new doors. These doors remain closed until a decision is made. Use the following steps to help you open new doors.

Step #1. WHAT IS THE PROBLEM?

Clearly define and analyze your EXACT PROBLEM. Write it down along with all of the symptoms. Trying to get the facts before defining the problem is just spinning your wheels. Boil it down to one specific problem. Too many people have found the *right answer* . . . but to the *wrong problem.*

USE EXPANDED THINKING. The problem is: Draw only four straight continuous lines and draw the lines in such a way that they go through all nine dots. . . .

It can be done by using expanded thinking. Break "mental barrier" thinking and go beyond what looks to be boundries:

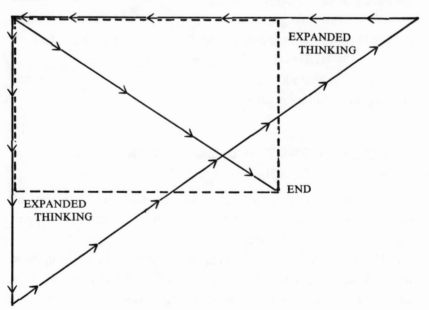

Step #2. WHAT ARE THE CAUSES OF THE PROBLEM?

After you know the exact problem, you are now in a position to pinpoint the EXACT CAUSE or CAUSES of the problem. You cannot possibly logically determine any other problem-solving step until you know "What's causing the problem." Causes are the basis and start us thinking in terms of corrective measures . . . the possible solutions. This requires indepth thinking. However, I feel that the S-T-O-P formula applies very well in this fast changing, competitive world . . .

*S*top

*T*hink

*O*r

*P*erish

Step #3. WHAT ARE THE POSSIBLE SOLUTIONS?

Make a list of possible courses of action. Be creative and use your "Green Light," future-oriented thinking. At this point do not stop to evaluate your ideas. Keep going until you get many possible solutions.

Step #4. DECIDE ON THE BEST SOLUTION.

There are always two categories involved in making a decision: People and Things. Use the chart shown below to help you completely analyze every possible solution to help you determine the BEST SOLUTION.

List everyone and everything involved and affected by the solution across the top and list all the possible solutions on the left hand side. Carefully analyze every solution by the way that solution will affect each category: good; no good; fair. By breaking down every possible solution in that matter, you will very quickly find the best solution and be able to make the most intelligent decision possible.

Here you use your "Red Light," judicial, past-oriented type of thinking.

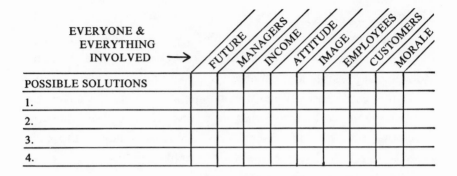

EVERYONE & EVERYTHING INVOLVED →	FUTURE	MANAGERS	INCOME	ATTITUDE	IMAGE	EMPLOYEES	CUSTOMERS	MORALE
POSSIBLE SOLUTIONS								
1.								
2.								
3.								
4.								

Step #5. IMPLEMENT THE BEST SOLUTION INTO ACTION.

Decisions are only made effective through action and effort. All the thinking and deciding doesn't do a thing until ACTION is taken.

When a person makes good decisions, has courage, doesn't procrastinate, then people trust, respect and have confidence in that person. When a person procrastinates and hates to make decisions, then people DO NOT trust, respect and have confidence in that person. Many times people feel very frustrated around the person who is about to "commence to begin" and has a bad case of PARALYSIS by ANALYSIS. *The quality of our decisions is a reflection of our abilities.*

BE WILLING TO RISK FAILURE TO SUCCEED

Many people DRIFT with the MEDIOCRE because it takes COURAGE, FAITH, PREPARATION, DESIRE and DETERMINATION to make DECISIONS, but the HAPPY, SUCCESSFUL ONE dares to ACT without hesitation on the best of the KNOWLEDGE, JUDGMENT, and INTUITION at that particular time. The person who deliberates too long is lost. FOR EVERY DECISION THERE IS A RISK, BUT AGAIN YOU MUST DECIDE.

ACT AND BURN THE BRIDGES BEHIND YOU and look forward to great expectations from the decision you have made. Once a decision is made, your mind is free to spend the thought and energy necessary to bring about the desired results you want.

Sometimes we ask ourselves—"How much will it cost me to make this decision?" Maybe we should ask—"How much is it going to cost me NOT to make this decision?"

NO SUCH THING AS JOB SECURITY

We hear a lot these days about job security. There is no such thing! If a person doesn't have security deep down inside himself, he has no security. If a person's security is in a job and he loses that job, he has lost everything. He has nothing. He is wiped out. SECURITY and CONFIDENCE are built by SUCCESSFUL EXPERIENCES and the more decisions you make that are right, the more inner security and confidence you will have . . . the more you will be willing to let loose of the past and burn the bridges.

"THE EAGLE AND THE OYSTER"

When God made the earth, he made the oyster. When he made the oyster, he determined his total security. You see, the oyster lives in a shell and when any changes in his surroundings take place, he immediately adapts automatically. If he wants food, he just opens his shell and food rushes in and, in essence, the oyster has to do nothing for survival.

But, on the other hand, God also made the eagle, a very rare bird indeed. He will invariably build his nest on the highest precipice he can find; he will fly through any weather to feed his young; fight any adversary to protect his family; and, as far as flight is concerned, his bounds are almost limitless.

The Eagle, not the Oyster, is the symbol of America, and the only way this image can be perpetuated is for you to stand up for your country and your profession. Make decisions for yourself and do the things failures don't like to do!

In 1944, I started working for the Union Pacific Railroad Company as a station helper-clerk. I went from a telegraph operator to a station agent, tour escort, train dispatcher and then to the marketing department in Chicago, I had all kinds of so called "job security"; regular salary, pension plan, health insurance, the whole works! I had everything but what I wanted . . . a job I loved.

In 1959, (I had thought the whole thing over for years that's why I can write this book), I finally got the COURAGE to make it on my own through my own efforts, brains and production. That's when I began to understand life, to live. I left 15 years of "security" for a straight commission selling opportunity (I didn't say job). Friends and job associates all thought I was nuts! I heard the negatives, "He'll never make it," "He'll be back in a year," but I knew some of the right things to do at that time and I did them. I started making more money the first year on the straight commission job than I did the last two years put together on the "security job."

I HAD MADE A DECISION AND DID NOT TURN BACK and I'll tell you that things didn't always go well then. I still have my share of challenges yet today, but I look forward to the opportunity of solving them. My attitude is "BE THANKFUL FOR PROBLEMS—THEY HELP US GROW."

HAS YOUR JOB GOT YOU?

It is always a pleasure to be around men and women who MAKE THINGS HAPPEN. They are the men and women who the JOB HAS . . . not men and women WHO HAVE A JOB and there's a big difference.

As many successful leaders have told me, "I want a person who is having a love affair—a love affair with his job!" Too many people get up in the morning and aren't EXCITED about LIFE and the OPPORTUNITIES of the DAY. They haven't learned how to live in a SUCCESSFUL PATTERN and one of the first requirements is to THINK, DECIDE, and ACT for YOURSELF. Be determined to decide to be the BEST of whatever you are.

> If you can't be a pine on the top of the hill,
>   Be a scrub in the valley—but be
> The best little scrub by the side of the rill;
>   Be a bush, if you can't be a tree.
> If you can't be a bush, be a bit of the grass,
>   And some highway happier make;
> If you can't be a muskie, then just be a bass—
>   But the liveliest bass in the lake!
> We can't all be captains, we've got to be crew,
>   There's something for all of us here.
> There's big work to do and there's lesser to do
>   And the task we must do is the near.
> If you can't be a highway, then just be a trail,
>   If you can't be the sun, be a star;
> It isn't by size that you win or you fail—
>   Be the best of whatever you are!
>   —*Douglas Malloch*

BIGGER PROBLEMS—MORE RISK—GREATER REWARDS

The bigger we grow and become, the larger are the problems and challenges we are required to solve. There is more risk involved, but also far more rewards waiting at the other end of the line. You can tell the SIZE of the PERSON by the SIZE of the PROBLEMS and CHALLENGES that person is able to cope with and solve. Problems—Risk—and Rewards all go together. When one is larger, the other two will automatically be larger.

MAKE DECISIONS THAT ARE NEITHER
PREMATURE—NOR TOO LATE

There is an old Persian proverb that goes, *"A stone thrown at the right time is better than gold given at the wrong time."*

One of the characteristics of good leadership is the act of doing things at the right time—making decisions that are neither premature, nor too late.

An excellent example of faulty leadership based on the wrong timing occurred in the Battle of Gettysburg. The battle lasted only three days and is considered by most military historians to be a classic example of *"How Not To Lead."*

Generals from both sides made mistakes, but one ill-timed decision in particular occurred on the very first day. The Union Army had been driven from its position on Seminary Ridge and was retreating in considerable disorder. The Confederates were chasing them, even though they themselves were pretty tired.

The Yankee's hope was for a break in the action and a chance to regroup on nearby Cemetery Ridge where they could set up a defensive position. It was four o'clock in the afternoon, leaving another four hours of daylight—plenty of time for the Southerners to rout the Northern army then and there.

This was not to happen, however, because of one man, Lt. General Richard S. Ewell, Commander of the Second Army Corps for the Confederacy. He had three whole divisions under him, two of which were fresh. Had he turned these divisions loose on the Union Army that afternoon when they were in flight, he would certainly have kept them off balance, and probably would have routed them then and there. He could then have turned and dealt with Meade who was still twelve miles away.

What happened? General Ewell sat on the ground under an apple tree mulling the situation over. Finally, unable to make up his mind whether to pursue or not to pursue, he decided to take the easy way out and mount his attack the following morning. This, of course, allowed the Union Army to regroup and eventually win the battle. Ewell's golden moment passed forever!

MAKE YOUR POSITIVE DECISIONS NOW

Don't talk about them—do them NOW. If indecision has a hold on you, break the negative habit right now, today. If you don't, you'll still hold the wrong type of mental picture about yourself. You'll attract the negative conditions around you that you would really like to rid yourself of and you'll probably be "upset" and "unhappy" for the rest of your life. The decision is up to you.

▲   ▲   ▲   ▲

"GARDLINES" *by Grant G. Gard*

DON'T TALK ABOUT THESE THINGS—DO THEM NOW!!

1. DECIDE exactly what you want from life.
2. Be determined never to use the statement "I CAN'T MAKE UP MY MIND."
3. Make DECISIONS PROMPTLY on good, sound information.
4. Look for the SIMPLEST SOLUTION to bring about adequate results.
5. Be willing to RISK FAILURE to succeed.
6. Create POSITIVE, DECISIVE MIND PICTURES and put them into ACTION immediately.
7. Let "ACTION" be your key word.

8. Fully understand that "IF IT'S GOING TO BE—IT'S UP TO ME."
9. Do your OWN DECISION MAKING without procrastination.
10. BURN your bridges behind you.
11. Use the 5 Steps to help you make EFFECTIVE DECISIONS and SOLVE PROBLEMS.
12. Realize that the quality of your decisions reflects your ABILITIES.

▲   ▲   ▲   ▲

THOUGHT PROVOKING QUOTES

"The men who try to do something and fail are infinitely better than those who try to do nothing and succeed."
—Lloyd Jones

"Not to decide—Is to decide."
—Harvey Cox

"Strong beliefs win strong men and then make them stronger."
—Walter Bagehot

"So long as I am acting from duty and conviction, I am indifferent to taunts and jeers. I think they will probably do me more good than harm."
—Sir Winston Churchill

"You will never "find" time for anything. If you want time you must make it."
—Charles Buston

"I pity the man who can travel from Dan to Beersheba, and cry, " 'Tis all barren''—and so it is, and so is all the world to him who will not cultivate the fruits it offers."
—Laurence Sterne

"Nothing can work me damage except myself. The harm that I sustain I carry about with me, and am never a real sufferer by my own fault."
—Saint Bernard

"Ask, and it shall be given you; seek and ye shall find; knock, and it shall be opened unto you."

—Matthew 7:7

"It is not a question of how much a man knows, but of the use he makes of what he knows; not a question of what he has acquired, and how he has been trained, but of what he is and what he can do."

—Josiah G. Holland

"Take all the swift advantage of the hours."

—William Shakespeare

"We ought not to look back unless it is to derive useful lessons from past errors, and for the purpose of profitting by dear-bought experience."

—George Washington

"When possible make decisions now, even if action is in the future. A reviewed decision usually is better than one reached at the moment."

—William B. Given, Sr.

"We ought to weigh well what we can only once decide."

—Publilius Syrus

"Our greatest glory is not in never falling, but in rising every time we fall."

—Oliver Goldsmith

"Know the true value of time! Snatch, seize and enjoy every moment of it. No idleness, no laziness, no procrastination. Never put off till tomorrow what you can do today."

—Lord Chesterfield

14 | *The Triangle of Successful Selling*

Everyone Sells. Everyone, regardless of occupation or profession, has something to sell. A person's success in life depends on how well he or she can get THEIR POINTS ACROSS. Sell yourself, sell your ideas, services, concepts or products. A person who does a good job of *persuading others* to his or her way of thinking *always gets to the top.*

The doctor sells patients, the lawyer sells the client, the minister sells the church, parents sell their children, just as much as the professional salesperson sells a product or service.

ENRICH THE LIVES OF OTHERS

Have you ever noticed that the man or woman who is influential with people is always "magnetic?" They are constantly selling themselves, bringing others over to their way of thinking, selling their ideas. They are known as the people who "really get things done" and "keep things moving." They are the people in the upper income brackets, gaining important recognition and living a "rich" life because they are able to *enrich the lives of others.*

They are the ones who receive the promotions and earn top incomes because they get desired results in dealing with people and get maximum production from their efforts. Why? They understand *people motivation* and *selling skills.* They know how to *turn people on!!*

SELLING—THE PROUD PROFESSION

Selling is the Proud Profession. It is an opportunity (I didn't say chance) for people to do their own thing. It is the most *lucrative* and *challenging* profession of all. It's all in how you handle it . . . because it has opportunity and potential unlimited. Selling is a profession just as much as being a dentist, medical doctor, lawyer, etc., is a profession. Why do I say "Selling is the proud profession"? . . . because you not only use it as a tool to achieve *your goals,* but also as an opportunity to be of REAL SERVICE TO MANKIND.

I frequently ask salespeople, "How many of you still have the first dollar you have earned from your first sale?" No hands go up. "How many of you know of people still enjoying the benefits of the service or products from your first sale or two?" Many hands go up.

So who is the winner in the selling profession? The BUYER . . . because he is ENJOYING THE BENEFITS of your product or service long after the commission dollars have been spent. BE PROUD TO BE A SALESPERSON.

Selling is a business so professional that half-sales don't count. Near hits don't mean a thing. A person either gets the order or not. Selling is a profession where years in the business have very little to do with a person's success. I've seen people in the selling profession with only six months experience completely outshine people with 5 or 10 years experience.

Why? Because they have learned to do the right things right, with the right people . . . at the right time to obtain the right results . . . they got the order. They didn't leave selling to chance. *They prepared themselves to capitalize on opportunities.* They know that a man will not accomplish anything greater than that which he is.

Many times I hear salespeople say, "I'm a good salesperson, but I am a poor closer" . . . or . . . "I have a hard time closing." If a salesperson is having a hard time closing or is unable to close, they are really saying, "I AM A POOR SALESPERSON," because the close is just a logical summation to a good selling presentation. The close is not just some *magical trick* that a select few know how to make happen.

Selling is an INDIVIDUAL EFFORT and those who make it truly a PROFESSION always end up making the most money. They close the highest percentage of prospects and they do not sell accidentally. However, it is reported that 80% of all sales made in this country are made ACCIDENTALLY. The salesperson cannot tell you, psychologically, why the sale was made or why the sale was lost. A person has to understand professional selling skills in order to *analyze* why he or she is making those sales.

It goes back to the old expression—"You can't play in the ball game if you don't know the rules." Selling is similar. I am afraid that too many people get into selling because "If they can't do anything else, they can always find a job selling." They look at selling as a last resort-type thing. When we are asked the question, "What do you do for a living?" we should SAY WITH PRIDE, "I'M A PROFESSIONAL SALESPERSON." We should always handle our profession, regardless of what it is, in such a way that we take a great deal of pride in what we are doing.

PROFESSIONAL SELLING—A LEARNING PROCESS

There is no one best way to sell a product . . . but there is a "one best way" for a person to sell and yet the average salesperson lives and dies and never finds it. Too many people feel that salespeople are "born." I have never looked in the birth column of the newspaper and read where a salesperson was born.

Salespeople are developed through the learning process just as in any other profession. Professional selling is a continual learning process. School is never out for the Pro. It is important, therefore, that the salesperson has a deep, burning desire for additional information with which to increase effectiveness.

Salespeople must have OPEN MINDS and be willing to ACCEPT and TRY OUT new ideas. The difference between the highly successful salesperson and the one who is just "struggling along" is primarily the difference in the skills that are used in doing the job.

The rest of this Chapter will be an outline for you to follow that consists of a few simple, professional selling skills. I believe that you must develop and sell according to your own personality. *No two salespeople sell the same way.* So use this outline and develop it in your own individual way so that you feel comfortable and confident.

What salespeople need is not a library full of psychological mumbo-jumbo, but they need a *few basic principles* that they can understand and use professionally. Study and get the following basic techniques committed to memory. Have an OPEN-MINDED ATTITUDE and realize that *good results* will come. Practice these principles daily until they become habits. It may be necessary for you to draw parallels with the points that I mention.

Regardless of your occupation, all of the principles mentioned in this Chapter can be used to help make you even more effective in winning friends, progressing in your job, getting the things that you really want in life and will help you become the type of person you want to become.

THE TRIANGLE OF SUCCESSFUL SELLING

I have found that salespeople progress on the basis of a TRIANGLE. The more skilled they become in the following three areas, the larger the triangle and more sales they make. Let's start with the bottom leg of the triangle which is PRODUCT KNOWLEDGE.

PRODUCT KNOWLEDGE

KNOW ALL YOU CAN ABOUT YOUR PRODUCT . . . Product knowledge makes up one leg of the triangle, but *only* one leg. It is vital. You should be able to answer any question that the prospect might ask you. PRODUCT KNOWLEDGE BUILDS YOUR SELF-CONFIDENCE just knowing that you can handle and explain any feature about your product.

The prospect has to LIKE YOU, TRUST YOU, BELIEVE YOU, RESPECT YOU, and ADMIRE YOU. If you cannot handle the questions about your product, the prospect will lose confidence in you, will not respect you and will go to a competitor, thus creating a BAD IMAGE FOR YOU AND YOUR COMPANY. YOU HAVE TO EARN YOUR PROSPECT'S BUSINESS.

ONLY ONE CHANCE TO MAKE A GOOD FIRST IM-PRESSION . . . You have only one opportunity to make a good first impression but if it is a poor impression, you may never be able to overcome the black mark. You have to stay in CONTROL and be CREATING A FAVORABLE IMAGE ALL THROUGH THE INTERVIEW. The other two legs of the triangle will help do this, but being armed with PRODUCT KNOWLEDGE certainly helps, also.

The buyer who knows the merchandise is tough on the salesperson who doesn't.

DO YOUR HOMEWORK! Yes, make it a *must* to study and dig up everything that you can about your product and your competitors' products, so that you can BECOME AN AUTHORITY AND A PROFESSIONAL IN YOUR FIELD. This builds "self-assurance" and removes "self-doubt." Failures don't take time to do this.

Successful salespeople do not overlook anything. They realize that there is NO SUCH WORD AS "LUCK." You build sales and product knowledge helps you to know the END USE, the END RESULT and the END BENEFIT that the prospect will receive from purchasing your product. Also, by knowing your product from A to Z and the benefits the prospect will receive from it, it will help you bring into balance the right amount of LOGIC with the right amount of EMOTION in your selling.

LOGIC AND EMOTION . . . Balance the logic and emotion in your selling. *You tell from the head, you sell from the heart.* Emotion unlocks the sale and logic locks it in. If the mind doesn't accept the product, the heart usually won't buy, and if the heart doesn't accept, the mind won't buy.

I have seen salespeople go into a selling interview and use all logic and no emotion. Three hours later, they ask for the order and nothing happens. They left the best educated prospect that they could. They taught the prospect well, but there was NO

EMOTIONAL COMMUNICATION and MOTIVATION in the interview and so nothing happened.

On the other hand, I have seen salespeople go into interviews and get all emotionally wrapped up with very little, if any, LOGIC (education) and make the sale, but the next day the phone rings and we have "buyer's remorse" on our hands . . . the prospect wants to back out.

The prospect bought on emotion with no logic and when he started to think it over, he didn't have enough facts to convince him that he did the right thing. ALWAYS BALANCE THE USE OF LOGIC AND EMOTION. It will cut down back-outs and buyer's remorse.

PRODUCT KNOWLEDGE ONLY PART OF THE SELLING PROCESS

Product Knowledge is certainly very important, but it is not the sole answer to successful selling. Last week, I heard a salesman say, "I'll get all the product knowledge that I can and then I'll be able to sell."

Not so! If product knowledge was the sole answer and all salespeople in your industry had the same amount of product knowledge, then everyone would be making the same number of sales, the same amount of commissions, etc. THIS IS NOT HAPPENING.

Let's face a fact and that fact is: All salespeople in your company or industry can learn the same amount of product knowledge, provided that they have the ABILITY, AMBITION and DESIRE to take the time and effort necessary to obtain this information. PRODUCT KNOWLEDGE BY ITSELF USUALLY SELLS ABSOLUTELY NOTHING.

I like the words of the vice-president in charge of sales for a leading life insurance company who said, "You can be a walking actuary, a walking encyclopedia in the insurance business and starve to death. We have thousands of people doing it every day. They know all of the facts, figures, events, contracts, riders, etc., and they still can't sell for sour apples."

The point that I am getting at is that you can know everything there is to know about your product and services and still fail as a Pro unless you apply the next two legs of the Triangle successfully.

The second leg of the triangle is MOTIVATION. A lot of our motivation comes from our attitude. I have covered attitude in the previous chapters—ways to shape your attitude into a WINNING ATTITUDE. Now I'll cover what motivates you and the prospect.

First . . . *Understand yourself.* Have you really sat down and figured out what motivates you? Here's a simple idea that works:

Take a sheet of paper and number down 1 through 10 on the left hand side of the page (example below) leaving some space between each number. Now beside each number list your greatest achievements. These achievements should be ones you are really proud of. They can come from hobbies, church work, your job, sporting events . . . just anything that you consider a real accomplishment.

Starting with #1, analyze what it was that caused you to

do that particular thing; what it was that motivated you into action. Was it PRIDE, PROFIT, LOVE, FEAR or SELF-PRESERVA-TION? Those are the five major motives. There are many sub-motives, but to keep it simple, we will deal with only the basic five.

When you have finished writing the motives in, you will find that one of the five has been used more frequently than the others. The one motive that caused the most action on your part is your DOMINANT MOTIVE. As a result of this exercise, you will have a better understanding of motives and the causes of action in yourself. Therefore, it will be much easier to find the motives in others.

```
1. Accomplishment:
   Motive:
2. Accomplishment:
   Motive:
3. Accomplishment:
   Motive:
4. Accomplishment:
   Motive:
      etc.
```

Take the same list of achievements and have your spouse fill in the motives as he or she sees you. Get his or her ideas as to what turns you on. Discuss it—compare it—talk about motives. Memorize the five major motives. You are now beginning to better understand what motivated you and what will motivate other people. Buyers are not the same . . . they can all be poured into the same mold, but they will NEVER come out the same. That is also true about salespeople. We must determine everyone's dominant motive on an individual basis. This is being creative.

IDEAS

There is only one word in the dictionary that will produce motivation. This is a key word for a salesperson. That key word is IDEAS. Before anyone moves or takes any action in any matter, *action is always triggered by an idea.* Ideas are always the forerunners to action or non-action.

NO TWO PEOPLE ARE ALIKE. An idea which might cause me to act might be a deterrent to action for another person. Whether we act or choose not to act on a certain idea will depend on our personal makeup and the dominant motive inside of us. This is why I am stressing: *Understand the five basic motives in people;* and, *The only way to get positive action is to come up with ideas that relate to the prospect's motive.*

HOW TO DETERMINE MOTIVATING FACTORS . . . It is said, and I firmly believe, that professional salespeople are "professional problem solvers" or "professional question askers." We must not overlook the plain, simple truth and that is, WE ARE NOT IN A POSITION TO SELL ANYBODY ANYTHING UNTIL WE KNOW WHAT THEY WANT OR NEED. We are not in a position to supply the right "ideas" to cause the prospect to act until we know the exact problem or the end benefit wanted.

People buy for two reasons—WANTS and NEEDS—and there is a difference. I may need a laxative, but I don't want one!! I bought a Hammond Concorde Organ, I didn't need it, but I sure wanted it. We have to determine what the prospect needs or wants and simply WHY that prospect needs or wants it. How do we do this? By asking questions and letting the PROSPECT DO MOST OF THE TALKING. We must be GOOD LISTENERS and ANALYZE what the prospect is saying.

Someone asked me what I feel the biggest failure areas are in salespeople. I feel salespeople fail to *ask enough questions* so that they can INTELLIGENTLY come up with the right ideas to motivate and to sell the prospect and they fail to know *when* to ask for the order.

STOP—LISTEN—ANALYZE—THINK

Listen! Every time the prospect opens his mouth he is telling us something, if we'll just *listen* and *analyze.* I have never been refused information from a prospect if I go at it right and here is an example:

"Mr. Jones, we've had quite a bit of success in helping others solve (supply your prospect's problem). With the thought in mind of determining what we can or cannot do for you, do you mind if I ask you a few questions?"

THIS IS POWERFUL! It has to be done SINCERELY AND HONESTLY. Show the prospect that you are interested in him and in helping him solve his problems. Continually *ask* key questions, *analyze* the answers and *observe* the prospect: "Now as I understand, Mr. Jones, what you are looking for is. . . ." "Is this correct?" "What you want to do is. . . ." "Is this correct?"

Here is where your product knowledge will really come in. You are then in a position to talk convincingly to him. This will be covered later in this Chapter. Right now, let's stick with THE FIVE MOTIVATING FACTORS: PROFIT, PRIDE, LOVE, FEAR and SELF-PRESERVATION.

PROFIT. "Mr. and Mrs. Smith, people who are using our bookkeeping system have reported we have saved them 8% on their bookkeeping expenses, and as much as 12% on their tax liability."

"Mr. Doe, It's a proven fact that customers buy more merchandise in this new style display rack. It doesn't take up any more floor space than the old one and it gives you about 30% more display space, thereby helping you to increase your profits.''

PRIDE. "Mrs. Johnson, you will be the talk of the neighborhood with this first-class washing machine in your house. When people drop in to visit, you'll sure be proud of this machine. You'll get many compliments on your choice.''

"Mr. Jones, you'll sure feel mighty important driving this new automobile. People will look at you and you'll just radiate success all over.''

"Mrs. Smith, this new hairstyle will make you look ten years younger and people will congratulate you on wearing the latest style.''

LOVE. "Mr. and Mrs. Smith, this lovely home will provide you and your family with a great deal of enjoyment. Your children will really enjoy the recreation room. The whole house is really built for complete family enjoyment and living at its best. What a nice way to express your love for your family.''

"Mrs. Williams, this ring you are purchasing for your husband will certainly let him know your deep love and affection for him.''

FEAR. "Mr. and Mrs. White, this policy will take care of your children in the event something happens to you. You can certainly have peace of mind knowing that their future is secure.''

"Mr. Smith, this machine will provide your customers with the most up-to-date service and you do not have to fear that your competitors will be taking business away from you.''

SELF-PRESERVATION. "Mr. and Mrs. Smith, this savings plan will give you complete safety for your hard-earned capital and also ensure you an income when you retire.''

"Mr. Smith, this burglar alarm system will give you complete protection for your entire business assets so that your cash inflow will never be interrupted and you can always make a living."

USE EMPATHY

USE EMPATHY . . . Find the hot button. Keep probing and asking questions until you are sure that you have found the hot button or the real motive that people have in wanting the thing you are selling them. Try hard to see things from the other person's point of view and through the other persons' eyes.

It may be that you will have to go from one motive to another, feeling your way. But know that it has to be one of those five areas and, as I said, we are not in a position to sell anybody anything until we know the prospect's PRIMARY INTEREST (WHAT he wants) and DOMINANT BUYING MOTIVE (WHY he wants it).

When once you have determined what the prospect wants, his *P.I.,* it is a very simple matter to find out why he wants it, his *D.B.M.* After you know what he wants, use this simple phrase as a bridge: "Why is this important to you, Mr. Doe?" The prospect will automatically tell you his *D.B.M.* You must LISTEN and ANALYZE. This is why I have constantly stressed question asking.

Sometimes we can get valuable motive information before we meet the prospect. If this is the case, you should always take time to verify what you have been able to obtain and make sure it is correct! Many times you have to get all of the information necessary to sell the prospect after you are face to face with him. The main thing is to be sure you obtain the RIGHT information in order to satisfy the prospects' NEEDS or WANTS. This enables you to sell CREATIVELY and MOTIVATIONALLY.

We ask questions for the following reasons:

1. To VERIFY the information we obtained ahead of the time we are face to face with the prospect.
2. To OBTAIN information we do not have, but must have to find out the need and the want. Thus enabling us to determine PRIMARY INTEREST and DOMINANT BUYING MOTIVE.
3. To get the prospect's AGREEMENT and to get "YES RESPONSES."
4. To be sure we are selling intelligently TO THE RIGHT PERSON and TO THE RIGHT MOTIVE.
5. To tactfully CHANGE the prospect's thinking to our way of thinking. This is the mark of a Pro.
6. Because it will help us to SAVE TIME, the prospect's time, and will help us to close more quickly.
7. To show the prospect that we aren't just interested in the commission check, but we are SINCERELY interested.
8. To create the IMAGE of a professional.
9. To SELL RELATED PRODUCTS.

As our question asking time goes up, our selling time goes down.

The third leg of the triangle is SELLING SKILLS.

We have talked about the importance of PRODUCT KNOWLEDGE and the importance of knowing what MOTIVATES the prospect. Now let's complete the triangle by talking about selling skills.

The actual SALES TALK . . . Before beginning the actual sales talk, I have found that several points are necessary to check . . .

HAVE A WINNING ATTITUDE AND SEE YOURSELF MAKING THE SALE. Get a good mental image of yourself succeeding, never failing.

BE ENTHUSIASTIC. Above all else, give yourself a PEP TALK and get yourself enthusiastic over the benefits you can bring to this prospect.

DON'T COUNT DOLLARS. Don't worry about the commission dollars! If you work with your prospect and show a SINCERE INTEREST in the prospects' needs and wants and show the "How can I best be of service" attitude, the "I really care" attitude, the commission dollars will take care of themselves.

GIVE BEFORE YOU RECEIVE. Don't be concerned if you have to "give" a lot. The rewards will automatically take care of themselves.

KILL "I'M NOT INTERESTED"

THE APPROACH. The first step for you to take in the selling talk is the APPROACH in which you want to get the prospect thinking about the benefits that you can provide. You must open the prospect's mind and kill "I'm not interested."

At the time you approach your prospect, he or she is thinking of himself or herself and his or her concerns or activities. You must divert the thinking from "self" to you. Don't talk about yourself. The prospect doesn't care about you or the company you represent. *Your first job in the interview is not to sell the prospect on the idea of buying, but to sell the prospect on the idea of listening.* When you approach someone at his or her front door or office, the first thing on that person's mind is, "Why is this salesperson here and what can he or she do for me?''

You must also remember that prospects are not interested in the product itself. They are interested only in the end use and end results, THE BENEFITS, they will derive from your ideas or goods. Millions of drills are sold . . . not because folks want drills, but because they want holes!

With the thought in mind that we must first open the prospect's mind and get him or her to listen to us, we must EARN HIS OR HER ATTENTION. Unless you get the prospect's attention and the prospect's mind opened, you will never get to give the rest of your sales talk. Consequently, you will never write the order. I hope you will place great importance on this step because it MAKES YOU or BREAKS YOU.

Here are some very important ideas that will help you earn the prospect's attention:

1. State a NEW IDEA. "Mrs. Smith, I've got some new ideas I'd like to discuss with you . . . ideas that could possibly save you a lot of time, trouble and money in the planning of your estate. Is it convenient to talk about these ideas now or would it be better for me to come back this afternoon at two o'clock?'' You state that you have some new ideas and then state the benefits you can provide.

2. Arouse the prospect's curiosity. Use a MYSTERY-TYPE opener to get the prospect's attention.

3. Use a BIG NAME. Use the name of a big company or important individual who is using your services profitably.

4. Use the REFERRAL. "Your friend, Jack Smith, thought that you might be interested in how we were able to save him several hundred dollars annually and still provide him with adequate insurance coverage.''

5. Get the prospect's mind opened by giving some type of

service at no charge. You give HELPFUL IDEAS or SERVICES at no charge, such as: appraisals; adjusting present equipment; evaluating present programs, etc.

6. Many companies provide FREE SAMPLES or some other GIFT. If you use gifts, try to make them something different, odd, and/or exclusive.

7. Pay some SPECIFIC COMPLIMENT. Be sincere!

8. State some STARTLING STATEMENT such as: "I just left a gentleman's office who said we were able to increase his net profit 10% in the first 90 days that he used our communication equipment.

9. ASK A QUESTION bearing on a need that will get a "yes" response. "Mr. Smith, I'll bet you would be interested in a program that could increase the production of your salespeople, help your company to show more profit and make your job as sales manager easier. That's right, isn't it?"

10. If your product is such that you can build an attractive, eye-catching EXHIBIT . . . do it. You can use that exhibit as an excellent attention-getter.

Attention-getting statements do not have to be long and time consuming. In fact, they should be brief and right to the point. Never use the approach, "I just happened to be in the area," and, for goodness sake, don't start with an apology.

Pronounce your prospect's name correctly and present a very sharp, enthusiastic, personal approach. *Be someone worth listening to and display personal qualities that others want.* As I have previously stated, you only have one chance at a first impression. Never take your mind off your goal: TO OPEN THE PROSPECT'S MIND AND TO KILL "I'M NOT INTERESTED."

Now you are ready to make a statement to obtain information to sell the prospect, to find the problem or to verify the information you got ahead of time. A statement like: "Mr. Smith, we have had quite a bit of success in helping people solve (state the problem). In order to determine what we might be able to do for you or what we might not be able to do for you, do you mind if I ask you a few questions?"

Here, find out everything you possibly can because if you don't know what he wants and needs and what the problem areas are, you aren't in a position to sell him anything. You could make a brilliant presentation of your product or service, but until you have determined the exact need, want or problem, the prospect will never listen and you'll be wasting the prospect's time and yours. BE SURE THE PERSON YOU ARE TALKING TO IS THE *RIGHT* PERSON TO BE TALKING TO, THE PERSON WHO CAN MAKE THE DECISIONS.

Reassure the prospect . . . keep his mind open . . . "Mr. Smith, as I understand it, this is the problem or this is what you would like done." "Is that correct?" (Get his agreement.) Questions help guard against misunderstanding. Ask questions frequently.

AROUSE INTEREST

At this point, you have the prospect's mind opened and you know the prospect's Primary Interest and Dominant Buying Motive. The next procedure is to ASSURE THE PROSPECT EXACTLY OF THE THING THAT CAN BE ACCOMPLISHED.

You'll have to use the exact wording for your product that fits you personally and the product or service that you are selling. Then, "Mr. Smith, for an investment of . . ., you can have this . . ., which would mean a savings to you of $ . . . per month"; or, "Mr. Smith, you can have the (benefit) which will give you the (solution to his problem)."

This further arouses the prospect's interest. He or she is

probably wondering, "How is this going to be done?" or, "Gee, that sounds great, but I don't know if the salesperson can really do all this for me."

CONVICTION

You now are at the next step of the selling process and that is: You must CONVINCE the prospect that you can do the thing you claim and that he or she is justified in buying . . . *NOW!*

In this step, you have to satisfy four questions:

Is it a good product or idea?

Will it do what the prospect wants or needs done?

Is it worth what we are asking?

Is the prospect justified in buying it now?

PROOF IS PERSONAL. You must keep it SIMPLE and RELATED to the prospect. You can effectively satisfy the four major questions by a DEMONSTRATION, an EXHIBIT, stating FACTS followed by RELATED BENEFITS, EXAMPLES, A-NALOGIES, TESTIMONIALS, or STATISTICS. You must convince the prospect honestly, sincerely and without using misleading facts.

I would much rather see a salesperson undersell a bit than oversell—I would much rather see the buyer receive a bit more than what was promised than not receive as much. The buyer must believe you and trust you, so don't use wild, exaggerated claims. Buyers don't believe claims.

For example, "This house will cut your heating bill in two," or "This car will get better gas mileage than any other car on the road." Those are claims and buyers don't believe claims. *Buyers are persuaded only by facts, evidence and proof that applies to individual, prospect-related benefits.*

Always carry evidence and proof with you to back up the

claims and facts you present. (If you can prove a claim then it becomes a fact.) Always tag on the BENEFITS of the product you are selling at that time. Buyers buy only one thing—the end use and the end result or benefit of the product. TALK "BENE-FITS" all the way through.

Frequently ask, "Have I made myself clear?" to be sure that the prospect is with you. "Do you have any questions to this point?" Keep checking to be sure you are on the RIGHT TRACK. Everything must relate to this particular prospect and his or her needs, wants or problems.

TRIAL CLOSES

Many sales can be closed after sufficient conviction. To make sure as to how you stand with the prospect, you use a trial close. A TRIAL CLOSE asks for an opinion or a minor decision. In a CLOSE, you ask for a decision. You can ask for an opinion at any time during the interview.

"Mr. Smith, in your OPINION, does this sound like something that could benefit your company?" or, "Mr. Smith, in your OPINION, does Monday sound like a better shipping day or would Thursday work into your schedule better?" You are asking for an OPINION.

A TRIAL CLOSE is just like a "Buyer's Thermometer" . . . you stick it in the buyer's mouth and if it reads 50 degrees you know that the prospect is cold and you have missed his Dominant Buying Motive. You then must go back and ask more questions to get on the right track with your prospect.

If you get a favorable response, a reading of 150 degrees, stop talking and *go right into the close.*

BUYING SIGNALS

A BUYING SIGNAL is anything that the prospect says or does that indicates he or she has mentally accepted your proposal. Do not feel that you have to continue on with the rest of your sales material. If he or she gives an acceptance of the product, the service, by saying something like this: "This sounds real good to me" . . . or, "Can I get this by next Monday?" he or she is saying, "OK . . . write the order."

Many times new salespeople feel that they have to go all the way through the selling process before they can write the order. Not so! In fact, it may cost you the order. You may sell it and turn around and repurchase it from the buyer. This has been done many times by salespeople who do not use the TRIAL CLOSE or LISTEN and WATCH for BUYING SIGNALS.

Here are some physical buying signals or signals of satisfaction to watch for . . . signals that indicate that the prospect, in all likelihood, has made a decision:

1. Prospect rubs chin or scratches head.
2. Prospect starts nodding head in approval.
3. Prospect picks up guarantee card or instruction sheet and reads with interest.
4. Prospect becomes increasingly friendly toward you or the product.
5. Prospect listens more closely.
6. Prospect relaxes visibly. For example: Opens up his tight-fisted hands or breathes a "sigh of relief."

By listening and watching for buying signals, signals of satisfaction, and using trial closes, you assure yourself of closing the sale at the right time. THERE'S ONLY ONE TIME TO CLOSE THE SALE AND THAT IS WHEN THE BUYER IS READY TO BUY. When you hear a buying signal and/or get a favorable "hot" response to a trial close, you know you are in the right "psychological period" to close the sale.

CREATE DESIRE

It may be, however, that the prospect might be saying to himself at this time, "I like the idea, and I'm convinced that it is a good product with good benefits. HOWEVER, I really don't have a desire to buy it." *Obviously, we now must create DESIRE.* Here you paint a very vivid mental picture of the prospect using the product, enjoying it and benefitting from it.

To create real desire, your picture must make the prospect see himself or herself enjoying the benefits. You will have to be extremely sharp, using your imagination to point this picture in the prospect's mind, but it will work. Don't leave desire to chance. The prospect's mind may be doing this without you doing it for him or her, but it may not. In painting the word picture, you will have another opportunity to use the prospect's *P.I.* and *D.B.M.* because he or she must clearly see himself or herself enjoying the benefits of your proposition. As soon as you have painted the mind picture and created desire, immediately use a trial close and then a close!

THE CLOSE

The close is the last step of the selling process. Here are some effective methods for closing the sale:

THE CHOICE OF TWO . . . "Did you want 200 shipped or would you like the one percent discount and have 500 shipped?" The QUESTION CLOSE: The prospect says, "Can I get this in units of six?" You reply, "If you could get this in units of six, would you be willing to go ahead and order at this time?"

YOU can close on a MINOR POINT . . . "You did like the blue one best, didn't you?"

You might try the Ben Franklin WEIGH CLOSE. Take a sheet of paper and on one side list all the reasons for buying and on the other side list the ideas opposed to buying, making sure the reasons for buying far outweigh the ideas opposed to buying.

REASONS FOR	IDEAS OPPOSED

THE INSTRUCTIONAL CLOSE . . . "Mrs. Smith, exactly what words did you want included in the contract?"

THE SUGGESTIVE CLOSE . . . "I suggest, Mrs. Smith, that you go ahead with an order of 12. This will give you some on hand and be a fair test for this new product." Remember, to close, you have to have the buyer's complete trust.

OBJECTIONS

Many salespeople take a personal affront when a prospect brings up an objection. You should look at objections as being good . . . a request for more information. There are several different kinds of objections. There is the HOPELESS OBJEC-TION . . . If it is a hopeless situation, don't waste any more of your valuable time on this situation. I know that many salespeople cling to this dead timber, trying to make something out of nothing.

There is the STALL. This gets into "I'll have to think it over." You might try something like this: "I'm sorry, I didn't explain the product clearly. Let's sit down together and go over anything that you are in doubt about."

The TRIVIAL . . . THE SMALL, USUALLY MEAN-INGLESS, OBJECTION . . . Sometimes you answer it and sometimes you don't. Too many times salespeople answer the trivial objection, the little "molehill," and make a mountain out of it. It may open up a whole new can of worms and the sale can be lost. Think and Be Careful!

THE GENUINE OBJECTION . . . This objection must be answered before you will close the sale. It is a REAL and BLOCKING objection.

Also, there is the PREJUDICED objection, sometimes called the "built-in" objection. This is something that your prospect has heard which may or may not be true. This one requires the tact of a real human relations specialist to change the prospect's thinking.

There are four times that you should answer objections: At the time the prospect brings up the objection; later in the interview; never; or, before the objection is ever brought up.

Here are some effective ways to answer objections:

REVERSE IT. Make it work for you. For example: The objection comes up, "The price is too high." Reverse it . . . drop the word "too" and put a benefit on it. "Mrs. Smith, the fact that the price is high may be the very reason you should invest in this equipment. You do want a machine that is fully guaranteed for 10 years, don't you?" Try to turn objections into reasons for buying.

Sometimes the best way to handle the objection is to EXPLAIN IT AWAY. There are times you may want to ADMIT IT and times you may want to DENY IT. Continually keep asking WHY questions: "Obviously, Mr. Smith, you have a good reason for feeling that way. Do you mind if I ask what that reason is?" "Then if we could come up with a payment plan that would work into your budget, you would be in a position to complete the arrangements, is that correct?" Keep searching and try to SMOKE OUT the REAL, the BLOCKING, OBJECTION.

Use your judgment, but the "second effort," many times, pays Big Dividends. DON'T BE AFRAID TO ASK FOR THE ORDER and don't be afraid to dig deeply to find the real objection in the event your prospect says "No." Stay until you have at least three "Nos." It takes courage, but don't give up easily. Selling isn't easy and, at times, you have to use every resource available to get the order.

Remember, you went after the order when you made the call. That should be the goal. Don't go in with the idea that it's just a "visit" or just a "good will" call—you are after results—The Order!!

PROSPECTING

One of the best sources of prospecting is working through satisfied buyers. They are enthused about your product and they will want others to receive the same benefits. Many times they will call and make the appointments for you or at least introduce you on the phone so that you can make the appointment. You have to ASK.

Remember, you strongly believe in your product. You are offering a real service. Don't hesitate to ask your clients for names and to help you make appointments. ALWAYS GET REFERRALS from those just sold . . . then follow up.

Another way of prospecting is to talk to influential business-people. They may not buy the product or service themselves, but they are sure to know many qualified people. So cultivate them and they will give you help.

A good way of prospecting is to have non-competing sales-people supply you with good prospects. Exchange prospects with them. You meet other salespeople every day. Share prospects with each other. Friends throughout the country can, many times, put you in touch with qualified leads. Your neighbors can also do this.

Talk to people who you do your business with . . . Your insurance agent, doctor, dentist, attorney, clothier, grocer, barber, dry cleaner, filling station owner, banker, apartment manager, investment broker, real estate salesperson, etc. Also use Chamber of Commerce membership lists (if available), and service club lists for prospecting.

Prepare educational and inspirational talks and speak before the Chamber of Commerce, Rotary, Lions, Kiwanis, all types of service clubs and women's groups. They'll get to know you and you will get to know them. Be a good speaker, as you want to create a favorable image. Talk to high school groups. Get as much exposure as you can. Help with Little League Baseball and Football, Boy and Girl Scouts and be active in your church.

Ask for interviews on "talk" shows—sure they won't let you on to do a commerical, but, many times, you can make it an informative type "Question and Answer" show, letting people know the latest! Read the latest newspapers. Get names of new people coming into the area; change of personnel and management; new businesses; and new industry from the newspapers. Get your name in Newcomers' books. Advertise. Perhaps your company goes 50-50 with you on paid advertising.

Write business interest stories and get them published in the business section of newspapers or maybe in the local news section. Go down the street and talk to businesspeople. There is always "Cold Canvas" for residential areas and business areas. Ask relatives for names. Use new acquaintances, people you meet for the first time and get to know them—church groups, P.T.A.s, bridge parties, etc. Use the telephone book and city directory.

When I lived in Texas, I knew an insurance man who got prospects everytime someone moved to town. He would drive by at about lunch time and say something like this, "I know you folks are busy and don't have time to cook, so here's some lunch—chicken, french fries, coffee, with my best wishes for a happy stay in Lubbock." He would leave his card and be on his way. Guess where those peoole would buy their insurance!!

Be creative, think of ideas like that. Remember, you can't make a sale if you don't make a call! If a person isn't prospecting properly, it has to be one of two reasons: Either the salesperson doesn't have the "Self-motivation" or doesn't have the "Know-How." Both areas have been covered in this chapter.

KEEP IN CONTACT

One of the best ways to build a clientele is to keep in close contact with the customer. I have heard salespeople say, "I'm afraid to go back in." If that's your method of selling, that's up to you. But if a customer is properly sold through the balance of logic and emotion, that customer should be excited about the benefits you and your product have given.

I know that there are times, after the sale, that the customers doubt that they made the right decision. The best way to hold down buyer's remorse is to SELL THEM SOLIDLY by finding out what they want and why they want it and then show them how to obtain it.

I bought a new Mercury Marquis from Ray Braumbaugh of Pueblo, Colorado. Ray called me several times to find out how the new car was working; if it was performing properly. Guess what I got when I bought that new car? I not only got a new Marquis, but I also got Ray Braumbaugh in the package! Needless to say, when it's time to buy another car and I'm within 200 miles of Pueblo, you know where I'm going to buy that car.

USE THE TELEPHONE

Ray used the telephone to keep in contact with me. You can use the telephone to keep in contact with your clients. I have yet to have any other salesperson, be it car, clothing, furniture, insurance . . . I don't care whatever . . . call me to show appreciation for my business and to see if the purchase was working out OK.

It takes time to do this, but it is well worth it for the good feeling that it will create within you, as the salesperson, and for the good it will create for the client. One of the ways for salespeople to stay HIGH and to OVERCOME DOWN DAYS is to remind themselves of the benefits of their product. So go out and service your accounts properly!

WRITE APPRECIATION NOTES

Here is another way to give service after the sale: Within 48 hours after the sale, write a thank you note to your client. A "THANK YOU" Note should contain two basic qualities: "CONGRATULATIONS" on the decision to buy and "REASSURANCE" that a wise decision was made. Don't make this note a commerical! In fact, it should be HANDWRITTEN and be very SHORT and BRIEF.

BE SPECIFIC

Don't use the typewriter. The note should be handwritten (typewritten is better than no note at all), I found it to be more meaningful. Make it specific. Don't say "Congratulations on buying a new car." Say instead, "Congratulations on your wise decision to purchase a new MARQUIS. You'll have many trouble-free, enjoyable miles, but we'll be happy to handle any problems that might come up. We are as close as your telephone. Thank you for the opportunity of serving you." Again I caution . . . BE SPECIFIC, NEVER GENERAL.

DON'T LOVE 'EM AND LEAVE 'EM

NEVER BE TOO BUSY to show your clients your APPRECI-ATION. It takes only a few minutes to call or write to say a heartwarming "THANK YOU." It means so much to your clients, and, as Ben Franklin said, "We are the best to ourselves when we are kind to others."

Theodore Roosevelt lived as hurried a life as any one of us and, yet, on campaign trips, when he was hurrying from one person to another, from one place to another, he never left his private train without stopping to thank the engineer and fireman for a safe and comfortable trip.

We all get excited before the sale is made and during the time the sale is being made, but, too often, we cool off after the sale is made. Don't fall into that trap! Have built-in service and contact after the sale and build your clientele in a good, solid way. Never be too busy to show *SINCERE APPRECIATION* . . . *DON'T LOVE 'EM AND LEAVE 'EM.*

RESPECT TIME

YOU can make investments, bet on football games, basketball games, etc., and if you lose, you can usually quickly recover your losses. In many ways of life, you can recover from your losses. You can err in your judgment, but as long as you work hard and wisely, you can usually recoup your losses.

This is not so with TIME! Once it is gone, it can never be recovered regardless of your knowledge, application of knowledge and regardless of how wisely you work. You are allotted 24 hours per day and whether you use it wisely or waste it . . . once it is gone, you can't recover it. You can't buy it, beg it or even steal it. Once it is ticked off, it is gone forever.

86,400 SECONDS PER DAY

Waste 15 minutes per day and you waste 11 working days per year! Look at seconds as being money. Let's say $86,400 per day because there are 86,400 seconds in every 24-hour period. If it will help to get time into the proper perspective and the true value of time, ask yourself, "How would I invest $86,400 per day?" I am sure it would vary between home, work and pleasure, as well as investments for the future. Perhaps looking at time as a true FUTURE BUILDING TOOL, we may learn to respect time more.

I like to think that if you are going to KILL TIME, you should "WORK IT TO DEATH."

THE $25,000 IDEA

Early in Charles M. Schwab's career, he made a request of a consultant: "Show me how to make more effective use of my time and I will pay you anything reasonable." The consultant recommended that at the end of each day Schwab write down the most important things that he had to do the following day. Then list them in the order of their importance. Then each day, when he started work, he should give his attention and effort to the most important thing going from #1 to #2, etc.

Continue working each day DOING THINGS IN THE OR-DER OF THEIR IMPORTANCE. Even though you may never get the list completed, you will always be performing the most important work first and thereby getting the GREATEST AMOUNT OF DESIRED RESULTS from the time you have spent.

No greater formula for success can be written. Charles Schwab is reported to have sent the consultant a check for $25,000. He later said that this one single idea for time management was the most valuable lesson he ever learned in his career.

WHAT IS YOUR TIME WORTH?

Take a look at this chart and do some self-analyzing . . .

If You Earn	Every Hour Is Worth	Every Minute Is Worth	In a Year One Hour A Day Is Worth
$ 2,000	$ 1.02	$ .0170	$ 250
2,500	1.28	.0213	312
3,000	1.54	.0256	375
3,500	1.79	.0300	437
4,000	2.05	.0341	500
5,000	2.56	.0426	625
6,000	3.07	.0513	750
7,000	3.59	.0598	875
7,500	3.84	.0640	937

If You Earn	Every Hour Is Worth	Every Minute Is Worth	In a Year One Hour A Day Is Worth
8,000	4.10	.0683	1000
8,500	4.35	.0726	1063
10,000	5.12	.0852	1250
12,000	6.15	.1025	1500
14,000	7.17	.1195	1750
16,000	8.20	.1366	2000
20,000	10.25	.1708	2500
25,000	12.81	.2135	3125
30,000	15.37	.2561	3750
35,000	17.93	.2988	4375
40,000	20.49	.3415	5000
50,000	25.61	.4269	6250
75,000	38.42	.6403	9375
100,000	51.23	.8523	12500

I suggest keeping a log for a month and honestly looking at each area of your day. Analyze and create ways to make better use of your time. I don't know of a single leader, businessperson or salesperson who can't be even more productive if he or she will make better use of time.

BE BUSY AND ORGANIZED

Plan your time and plan your day by doing the MOST IMPORTANT THINGS FIRST and refuse to let the minutes go by without making them pay. When you are using time to its greatest advantage . . . you are BUSY and ORGANIZED. People like to do business with and work for a BUSY and ORGANIZED person. It certainly helps to create that POSITIVE IMAGE and IMPRESSION—*It's Working Wisely.*

In summary, Professional Selling involves all 3 legs of the triangle, which we have covered in this Chapter. Make your SELLING TRIANGLE GROW by learning more Product Knowledge, Motivational Knowledge and Selling Skills everyday.

PRODUCT KNOWLEDGE

WHERE YOU ARE NOW
WHERE YOU WILL BE ONE YEAR FROM NOW

▲ ▲ ▲ ▲

"GARDLINES" *by Grant G. Gard*

DON'T TALK ABOUT THESE THINGS—DO THEM NOW!!

1. Be DETERMINED and PROUD to be a "professional" salesperson.
2. Get ALL the PRODUCT KNOWLEDGE you can.
3. Be determined to know EVERY BENEFIT your product offers.
4. Secure interested ATTENTION and OPEN PROSPECT'S MIND . . . killing "I'm not interested."
5. ASK QUESTIONS in order to become a professional problem solver.
6. Be determined to be believable by producing CONVINCING EVIDENCE.
7. Sell BENEFITS and END RESULTS.
8. Always create strong DESIRE for your product by making the prospect see the benefits in his mind.
9. Always ASK for the order.
10. Don't be afraid of OBJECTIONS (turn them into reasons for buying).

11. Be a good LISTENER and ANALYZER.
12. "EARN" your prospect's business.
13. LISTEN for Buying Signals and USE Trial Closes so you will know when to close the sale.
14. Understand that you can close the sale ONLY when the prospect is ready to buy.
15. Memorize the Buying Motives and sell motivationally—APPEAL to motives that make people act.
16. Always be OPTIMISTIC regardless of a turn down.
17. Always make a good impression by having the prospect LIKE, BELIEVE, TRUST, RESPECT and ADMIRE you.
18. Constantly "PROSPECT," realizing new business is the "life" of your business.
19. WIN the confidence of the prospect by your confidence, your belief and your sincerity in your product.
20. Use a balance of LOGIC (Education) and EMOTION.
21. BE ORGANIZED. Make time pay dividends.
22. Don't love 'em and leave 'em. SHOW APPRECIATION.
23. Give yourself PEP TALKS. *Sell enthusiastically.*

▲　▲　▲　▲

THOUGHT PROVOKING QUOTES

"Talk to a man about himself and he will listen for hours."
　　　　　　　—Benjamin Disraeli

"Be wiser than other people—if you can; but do not tell them so."
　　　　　　　—Lord Chesterfield

"One thing I know: The only ones among you who will be really happy are those who will have sought and found how to serve."
　　　　　　　—Albert Schweitzer

"When God wanted sponges and oysters, He made them and put one on a rock, and the other in the mud. When He made man, He did not make him to be a sponge or an oyster. He made

him with feet and hands and head and heart and vital blood, and a place to use them and said to him, 'Go Work!' "
—Henry Ward Beecher

"One of the chief reasons for success in life is the ability to maintain a daily interest in one's work, to have chronic enthusiasm, to regard each day as important."
—William Lyon Phelps

"Work is the true elixir of life. The busiest man is the happiest man. Excellence in any art or profession is attained only by hard and persistent work. Never believe that you are perfect. When a man imagines, even after years of striving that he has attained perfection, his decline begins."
—Sir Theodore Martin

"God intends no man to live in this world without working, but it seems to me no less evident that He intends every man to be happy in his work."
—John Ruskin

"An enterprise, when fairly once begun, should not be left till all that ought is won."
—William Shakespeare

"Do a little more each day than you think you possibly can."
—Lowell Thomas

"Experience shows that success is due less to ability than to zeal. The winner is he who gives himself to his work, body and soul."
—Charles Buxton

"You will never stub your toe standing still. The faster you go, the more chance there is of stubbing your toe, but the more chance you have of getting somewhere."
—Charles F. Kettering

"Life is a lively process of becoming. If you haven't added to your interest during the past year; if you are thinking the same thoughts, relating the same personal experiences, having the same predictable reactions—rigor mortis of the personality has set in."
—General Douglas MacArthur

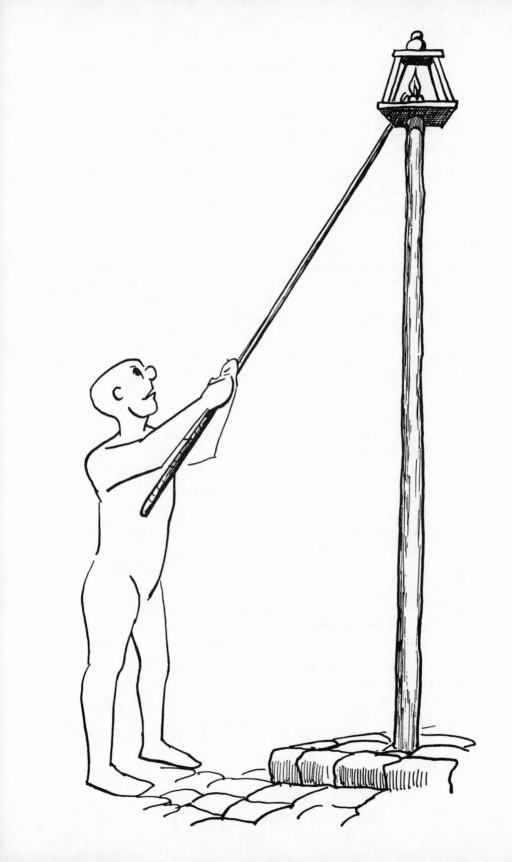

How to Remember Names and Things . . . Easily

15

Light the Lights in Others. Have you ever noticed that the man or woman who can remember peoples' names stands head and shoulders above everyone else? The person who can do this is "lighting up" the other person. The deepest craving we have is to feel important. When people call us by name, we know they are SINCERELY INTERESTED IN US and we aren't just a number, a *nobody*. They make us feel *important,* like a *somebody*.

LAMPLIGHTER

There was an old lamplighter who lived in a village. Each evening, at dusk, he would go and gather the tools of his trade. He would start to make his way up the street, lighting the lamps as he went. He would go to the first lamp pole, place his ladder, climb up the ladder and remove one of the panes of glass. He would then clean all of the glass, trim the wick and finally, after it was all ready, he would light the lamp.

He would then climb down his ladder, pick it up, along with his other tools, and go to the next lamp. Lamp by lamp, light by light, he would make his way up the street, shining, trimming and lighting. Soon he would disappear over the hill and around the corner, but *you could always tell where he had been by the lights he had lit.*

I'm sure each one of you wants to be known as a terrific "people builder," lighting the lights in other people, so you can look back each day and feel that you have made a favorable contribution to other peoples' lives. Calling people by name is one way of doing exactly that . . . it's good *Human Relations* and good *Public Relations.*

SELL YOURSELF ON YOURSELF

The first thing you must do is *"sell yourself on yourself"* . . . you've got what it takes to do it.

Sell yourself on the *importance of remembering names.* By remembering peoples' names, it helps to:

Make people feel important.

Win customers and clients.

Keep customers and clients.

Practice the "Golden Rule" by doing unto others as we'd
    have others do unto us.

Prevent embarrassment.

Be more influential with people.

Warm people up—break barriers.

Put people at ease.

Gain recognition.

Be known as a real *people builder.*

Professor Carl Seashore said, "The average man does not

use above 10% of his inherited capacity for memory. He wastes
the 90% by violating the natural laws of remembering."

The three natural laws of memory are very simple:

1. LISTEN AND OBSERVE
2. REPEAT
3. ASSOCIATE

LISTEN AND OBSERVE. The first requirement for remembering a person's name is to LISTEN TO THE NAME . . . hear
it clearly and OBSERVE THE INDIVIDUAL. Too much of the
time we are too busy thinking of ourselves to hear the name properly
or we are too self-conscious. If you are male, you are wondering
if your shoes are shined; if your suit is pressed. If you are female,
you are wondering if your hair looks OK; if the seams of your
hose are straight. We simply fail to take a SINCERE INTEREST
in the other person. To hear the name and to observe the person
demands complete concentration and the right type of "want to"
attitude.

Hear the name clearly. If the name is not heard clearly, ask
the individual to repeat the name. No one has ever been offended
when they have been asked to repeat their name. Say something
like this: "I'm sorry, I want to make sure I get your name right.
Would you please repeat it for me one more time?" Or perhaps
something like this: "Please repeat your name for me, I'd like
to get the spelling correct. I'll write it down as you spell it."

Seeing a thing just one time is worth a thousand words of
description, so writing out the name can surely help. Remember,
it is that person's name, that person's greatest possession. They
will gladly cooperate and feel honored to give it to you because
you are making them feel important. You can't expect to remember
the name if you've not heard it correctly.

Observe the person. Many times there is something about
the person's voice, their size, their face and/or their actions that

stand out and make it easy to remember the name with the person.

REPEAT. You can remember almost anything if you will repeat it often enough. Remembering names is easy if you will repeat them several times so that you engrave the name in your mind. Use the name as soon as you meet a person. "It's a pleasure to meet you, Mr. Doe." Keep using the name in conversation. Repeat it silently to yourself. Use it when you leave a person, "It's been nice meeting and visiting with you, Mr. Doe."

ASSOCIATE. Our minds are an Associating Machine. If you say that you have a bad memory, you are really saying, "I have a bad set of associations."

Use your imagination and make a mind picture in which you associate the name with something. For example, my name is Grant Gard. Here picture me in a "U.S. Grant" army uniform, applying lots of Right Gard spray deodorant. It may seem silly, but it works. In fact, the sillier, the more ridiculous and absurd the mind picture is, the easier it is to remember.

Association is the strongest bond we can use to remember names. *Become creative in building mind pictures.* That is the key. Sometimes you can use a similar name to help you recall the name . . . another person who has the same name. There might be something about the name that blends into the person's business. You will find, with practice, you can build absurd and ridiculous mind pictures that associate the name and make the name easy to recall whenever you "pop the picture" into your mind.

HOW TO REMEMBER THINGS

Using the mind picture and association techniques, you can easily remember items, objects, articles, groceries, or whatever. The key . . . MEMORY PEGS. Memorize the key word that rhymes with the number and develop a mind picture placing the "thing" you want to remember in the picture:

ONE—RUN. Visualize horses running and racing. Place the article, item, or object that you want to remember all over the horses. Sounds ridiculous, but it will work.

TWO—ZOO. Visualize the monkeys feeding *us* through the bars. Monkeys have in their hands the thing we want to remember, sticking it in our mouths.

THREE—TREE. Picture a huge Christmas tree. Place the object to remember all over the tree.

FOUR—DOOR. See a revolving door . . . spinning, coming out and hitting us is the thing we want to remember.

FIVE—HIVE. See a large bee hive . . . bees going up in the sky carrying the item to be remembered.

SIX—MIX. Picture mixing up a cake and article falls into the batter.

SEVEN—HEAVEN. See a plush, gold carpet going up to heaven. The thing we want to remember going right up the carpet and entering heaven.

EIGHT—GATE. See the long arm railroad gate carrying the thing to remember up and down on the gate.

NINE—WINE. See a large bottle of wine. Instead of pouring wine out, it pours out object to be remembered.

TEN—DEN. Visualize a lion in his den trying to escape and you throw the object to be remembered at the lion to keep him in the cage.

ELEVEN—FOOTBALL ELEVEN. See a football team with the quarterback throwing the article to be remembered to an end who catches it and takes it in for a touchdown.

TWELVE—SHELF. Place the object you want to remember on the shelf then have it drop to the floor.

THIRTEEN—HURTING. You hit your finger with the item to remember, causing the finger to bleed.

FOURTEEN—COURTING. See a couple on a park bench

trying to kiss and the item that you want to remember comes between them.

FIFTEEN—LIFTING. A strong man lifts the object way above his head and then drops it to the floor.

SIXTEEN—LICKING. You are boxing and on one hand you have a glove and on the other hand the object is strapped to your fist.

SEVENTEEN—LEAVENING. You are kneading bread dough and you knead the object you want to remember into the dough.

EIGHTEEN—WAITING. You are waiting for a bus on the corner. The doors open and out comes the object you want to remember.

NINETEEN—PINING. See a lady crying, but instead of crying tears she is crying the item to be remembered.

TWENTY—HORN OF PLENTY. Picture a huge horn of plenty swinging back and forth across the room and the thing we want to remember keeps falling out.

TWENTY-ONE—DUELING GUN. Two men fire their dueling guns, but instead of bullets, they fire the object to be remembered.

TWENTY-TWO—SHOE. Have the thing to be remembered in a pair of shoes.

TWENTY-THREE—KNEE. Picture the article you want to remember hitting and damaging your knee.

TWENTY-FOUR—FLOOR. See the object to remember falling and smashing on the floor.

TWENTY-FIVE—THIGH. Picture the article to remember hitting your thigh.

TWENTY-SIX—FIX. Using a hammer, drive a nail to fix the article you want to remember.

TWENTY-SEVEN—TWO SEVENS. Throw dice and they

come up "two sevens" and land right on top of article to be remembered.

TWENTY-EIGHT—SWINGING GATE. Place object to remember on a gate that is swinging open and closed.

TWENTY-NINE—SHINE. Rays of sunshine are pictured shining on the thing to be remembered.

THIRTY—DIRTY. Put the article that you want to remember into a small boy's dirty, grimy hands.

It takes practice. First, memorize the key words, memorize the picture for each key word and then all you have to do is put the "article—the thing you want to remember" into the picture. You'll find out that your "recall power" and your "memory" will be outstanding.

▲   ▲   ▲   ▲

"GARDLINES" *by Grant G. Gard*

DON'T TALK ABOUT THESE THINGS—DO THEM NOW!!

1. Develop your ability to CALL PEOPLE BY NAME.
2. Use MEMORY PEGS to help you remember articles or items.
3. PRACTICE the memory principles every day for continual memory improvement.

▲   ▲   ▲   ▲

THOUGHT PROVOKING QUOTES

"Goodwill is the one and only asset that competition cannot undersell or destroy."

—Marshall Field

"Think like a man of action, act like a man of thought."
—Henri Bergson

16 | *100 Steps to Achievement*

I have trained and spoken to thousands of executives, leaders, salespeople, farmers, housewives, and employees, men and women from all walks of life and I have compiled the following list from this question that they have asked, "What qualities have you observed in a highly successful person?"

This is the list . . . not in any kind of order of importance:

1. Doesn't blame others for things that go wrong.
2. Realizes that we create our own destiny and problems.
3. Is mature.
4. Always uses tact in all of his or her dealings with people.
5. Speaks with conviction.
6. Can pull himself or herself up after a slump or reversal.
7. Presents ideas with enthusiasm and animation.
8. Always is a well-groomed person.
9. Doesn't let "NOs" and obstacles get him or her down.
10. Radiates sincerity and integrity.

11. Has courage, self-confidence and has learned how to control fear.
12. Never exaggerates.
13. Utilizes good communications.
14. Always shows faith in his or her cause.
15. Is ambitious.
16. Constantly is improving himself or herself through books, tapes, seminars and lectures.
17. Analyzes his or her day and doesn't make the same mistake twice.
18. Knows how to get a point across effectively.
19. Can influence people on any level.
20. Speaks excellent grammar.
21. Uses empathy.
22. Has a spouse who really cooperates.
23. Has definite, written, well-defined, worthy goals and is always striving to achieve them.
24. Uses good judgment.
25. Plans presentations . . . leaves nothing to chance.
26. Makes every move look professional.
27. Always is optimistic.
28. Never argues.
29. Never displays too much confidence, never is the "know-it-all" type.
30. Always is very punctual—on time.
31. Is aggressive.
32. Always listens to other people's point of view.
33. Is patient with others who can't plan and understand as well as he or she can.
34. Prevents embarrassment . . . never criticizes in front of others.
35. Understands motivation of people.

36. Organizes all activities.
37. Calls people by name.
38. Doesn't bring domestic problems to work.
39. Makes sound decisions without procrastination.
40. Leads and "sells" by excellent example.
41. Has a good sense of humor.
42. Has a good self-image.
43. Builds everyone up to his or her level of excitement.
44. Is an excellent listener and observer . . . analyzes well.
45. Is believable and genuine.
46. Is always truthful.
47. Is persistent . . . never gives up.
48. Can overcome objections and complaints.
49. Can overcome stalling situations.
50. Knows how to find motives to turn others on.
51. Always displays a winning attitude.
52. Listens for any suggestions to improve himself or herself.
53. Thinks "BIG."
54. Practices self-discipline.
55. Makes a real good first impression.
56. Knows and understands his or her job well. Is a PRO.
57. Is a professional "question asker."
58. Never peddles gossip.
59. Communicates with a minimum of misunderstanding.
60. Does not oversell ideas.
61. Never drinks on the job.
62. Does things in the order of importance.
63. Takes good care of his or her health.
64. Is likeable and trustworthy.
65. Uses the balance of logic and emotion.
66. Does not tell off-color stories.
67. Looks, acts and talks like a winner.

68. Keeps current with local and national news so he or she can communicate intelligently.
69. Admits when he or she has erred.
70. Is "image-conscious."
71. Uses evidence to help convince.
72. Is flexible and accepts change.
73. Expresses ideas well in conversation and writing.
74. Never goes to pieces under pressure.
75. Always respects the dignity of the other person.
76. Never is intolerant and closed-minded.
77. Accepts responsibility.
78. Is dependable.
79. Uses first-rate business cards and stationery.
80. Keeps all promises and commitments.
81. Hand writes notes of appreciation.
82. Pays sincere compliments.
83. Fills out all paperwork and reports on time.
84. Takes an active part in company, civic, church and school activities.
85. Gives recognition for good ideas and suggestions.
86. Does not permit himself or herself to stagnate.
87. Is original . . . doesn't follow the beaten path.
88. Does not dwell on minor mistakes.
89. Listens to the emotional content of what others say.
90. Always displays high principles and high standards of conduct.
91. Is willing to go the "extra mile."
92. Displays initiative to the point of being a self-starter.
93. Has a real desire to find new and better ideas.
94. Inspires people . . . makes them "want to."
95. Uses time to the best advantage.

96. Is creative.

97. Looks at problems as opportunities to grow.

98. Is never satisfied with the status quo.

99. Knows how to open peoples' minds to accept his or her ideas.

100. Doesn't just talk about doing things but DOES THEM.

I am sure that you could add some more to this list, but take each one and use it as a check point for YOU. I know you will be strong in many areas, but you may find some areas to start working on today—RIGHT NOW!

▲ ▲ ▲ ▲

THE WORLD NEEDS MEN

. . . who cannot be bought;

. . . whose word is their bond;

. . . who put character above wealth;

. . . who possess opinions and a will;

. . . who are larger than their vocations;

. . . who do not hesitate to take chances.

. . . who will not lose their individuality in a crowd;

. . . who will be as honest in small things as in great things;

. . . who will make no compromise with wrong.

. . . whose ambitions are not confined to their own selfish desires;

. . . who will not say they do it "because everybody else does it."

. . . who are true to their friends through good report and evil report, in adversity as well as in prosperity.

. . . who do not believe that shrewdness, cunning, and hardheadedness are the best qualities for winning success;

. . . who are not ashamed or afraid to stand for the truth when it is unpopular, who can say "no" with emphasis, although all the rest of the world says "yes."

—Harold R. Nelson

▲   ▲   ▲   ▲

THOUGHT PROVOKING QUOTES

"The secret of success in life is for a man to be ready for his opportunity when it comes."

—Disraeli

"Many do with opportunities as children do at the seashore; they fill their little hands with sand and then let the grains fall through one by one until they are gone."

—Thomas Jones

"I'll study and get ready and be prepared for my opportunity when it comes."

—Abraham Lincoln

"It is not a question of how much a man knows, but of the use he makes of what he knows; not a question of what he has acquired and how he has been trained, but of what he is and what he can do."

—Josiah G. Holland

"Courage is the chief attribute to manliness."
—Daniel Webster

"Our fears are always more numerous than our dangers."
—Seneca

"Action may not always bring happiness, but there is no happiness without action."

—Benjamin Disraeli

"Take therefore no thought for the morrow; for the morrow shall take thought for the things of itself. Sufficient unto the day is the end thereof."

—Matthew 6:34

"To know what is right and not to do it is the worst cowardice."
—Confucius

"The older we get the more we realize that service to others is the only way to stay happy. If we do nothing to benefit others we will do nothing to benefit ourselves."

—Carl Holmes

"Do all the good you can,
By all the means you can,
In all the ways you can,
In all the places you can,
At all the times you can,
To all the people you can,
As long as ever you can."

—John Wesley

"To contrive is nothing! To construct is something! To produce is everything!"

—Eddie Rickenbacker

"The only real security I know of is a store of resourcefulness acquired by meeting trouble head on and looking it squarely in the eye."

—Danny Thomas

"The absent are never without fault, nor the present without excuse."

—Ben Franklin

"Practice does not make perfect; perfect practice makes perfect."

—Vince Lombardi

"Do the thing and you will have power."

—Emerson

"The greatest man in the world, in my opinion, is the man who can take an average job and make something of it."

—George Allen

"Keep your fears to yourself, but share your courage with others."

—Robert Louis Stevenson

"You can do nothing effectually without enthusiasm."

—Guizot

"Every production of genius must be the production of enthusiasm."

—Disraeli

17 | *Creative Leadership*

The ability to lead people and direct their energies toward DESIRABLE GOAL ACHIEVEMENT is a very significant factor in the success of men and women. The speed and growth and the eventual height reached by anyone and the monetary rewards gained will be determined by their effectiveness in leading others. No business, community, church or school will progress without leadership. John A. Patton said, "Ninety-nine percent of the people in this world want to be told what to do. Be the other one percent."

The opportunity to lead; to shape the lives of others; to provide an authentic service to people, communities, businesses and enterprises can be an experience equal in excitement and satisfaction to that offered by any profession. Take a new look at your leadership abilities, plot a fresh and creative approach to it and your future can be unlimited. Those leaders who know how to get *desired results through people* get to the top in any field of endeavor.

The following story was told to me and I pass it along as

a perfect example of what I am talking about:

Executive Vice President Jim Stevens: "I'm in favor of giving the promotion to Ronald Williams. He knows how to get others to work and how to build a team."

General Manager Raymond Hill: "I agree that Ronald is a good man, but he hasn't been with us nearly as long as several of the others who are expecting this promotion."

Mr. Stevens: "Raymond, you are probably right. But let me ask you, 'What do we spend the most money for around here?' Payroll—that's what takes the largest share of the expense dollar. Now, which one of the supervisors out there is getting the best return for those payroll dollars? Ronald Williams, that's who. Ronald has demonstrated during the past two years that he knows how to get along with people. He keeps his people satisfied, and what's more important, he has the top production department. His people are well trained; he has practically no turnover; he's firm, but they still think he's a great guy; he knows everyone in the department; he always seems to know how his people will react and exactly what they can be expected to do."

Mr. Hill: "Yes, when you put it that way, I begin to see what you mean."

Mr. Stevens: "What's more, a man who has done that kind of job is needed in a bigger job. He develops people and makes money for the company. We want more of both. Raymond, you talk with Ronald Williams and tell him that as of the first of the month he will be plant superintendent. Any man who can handle people the way he does deserves a bigger job. In the meantime, we'll have the necessary meetings to make the announcement."

It was in this manner, and for these reasons, that Ronald Williams became plant superintendent. He had been a foreman for only two years and was promoted over three senior foreman *because he knew how to get desired results through people.*

George Halsay summed up the idea best in *LEADING PEO-PLE* when he stated, "It has been demonstrated time and time again that almost any person of normal intelligence and sincere desire to be of service to people can acquire considerable skill in the art of leading people if he will study its principles and methods and then apply them thoughtfully, conscientiously and persistently."

Here are the characteristics and skills that enable people to do a good job of leading people, of getting desired results through people:

PLANNING. True leaders PLAN. Nothing is left to chance. They know where they are going, what it is going to take to get there and, because they have PURPOSE AND DIRECTION, others follow. They evaluate their present situation and understand the factors which will help and those which will hinder their efforts, so that they can set realistic, long range, intermediate and short term goals. They know that without careful planning and goals that they and everyone around them will be *task oriented* instead of *goal oriented.* The real leader knows that when you take your eyes off of the goal to be achieved, you become lost in the field of little details and tasks and therefore lose sight of results you want to achieve.

After you have determined the overall goals to be achieved, you must determine a definite plan of action and MAKE SURE that EVERYONE INVOLVED clearly understands the plan, the goals, and the part he or she plays in achieving the end results so that all concerned will act as a TEAM. Goals should always be broken down into "bite size pieces" so that no one feels overwhelmed by the magnitude of the entire long range results to be achieved.

You must set deadlines for yourself and your people for each phase of the program to make sure things are happening on schedule.

The true leader always *puts first things first* and never becomes blinded by the "details" and "tasks" which will prevent the achievement of the really *important goals.*

ORGANIZING. After the goals to be achieved have been determined, then the *real must* is to get the right person on the right job to obtain the right results by best *using that persons' finest skills and abilities.* Don't fall into the trap of fitting jobs to people when you should be fitting people to jobs!

Surround yourself with capable people. All successful leaders realize that they could not handle all the details that enable them to reach high goals and accomplishments all by themselves. The best leaders choose and organize capable people to help get the job done successfully. As the other peoples' contributions increase, leaders find themselves reaching higher levels of accomplishment.

The Chicago Tribune once called Henry Ford an ignoramus in print. Ford sued and challenged the paper to "prove it." During the trial Ford was asked dozens of simple, general-information questions: "When was the Civil War?" "Name the Presidents of the United States." And so on. Ford, who had little formal education, could answer very few.

Finally, exasperated, he said, "I don't know the answers to those questions, but I could find a man in five minutes who does. I use my brain to *think,* not store up a lot of useless facts."

A similar story is told about Einstein. Someone once asked him, "How many feet are in a mile." "I don't know," Einstein is reported as saying. "Why should I fill up my head with things like that when I could look them up in any reference book in two minutes."

Those two men, giants of the past, knew what every good leader learns sooner or later: The ability to get information, and then to *act on it* is what gets things done. As one business leader recently put it, "I want people around me who can solve problems, who can get things done, not recite facts."

DIRECTING. To get desired results from and through people, real leaders know that they must provide guidance and coaching. They are responsible for issuing the orders, directives, policies, instructions and procedures that will lead their people to goal achievement. In doing so, GOOD LEADERS know that they must involve their people in sharing the ideas and concepts which relate to their part of the total picture. Thereby, making them feel like they are a very vital and important part of the TEAM instead of just ORDER TAKERS.

Pros lead always by setting the right example. *They must first build into themselves what they want to see in their people.*

By involving their people and making sure that each member knows his or her part and that they feel important, a climate of cooperation is established. This keeps the MORALE HIGH and builds in a *"WANT TO" attitude in people.*

General Eisenhower used to demonstrate the art of leadership with a simple piece of string. He'd put it on a table and say, *"Pull it* and it'll follow wherever you wish. *Push it* and it will go nowhere at all."

It's just that way when it comes to leading people. If people don't follow a leader *voluntarily*—if the people always have to be pushed and forced—then they are not under the guidance of a good leader.

Effective leaders depend on their ability to make people *want to follow.* They work to inspire people, making them *want to cooperate.* They give the proper guidance and coaching to get the best efforts out of their poeple.

CONTROL AND FOLLOW UP. The effective leader always "keeps things moving smoothly" and "makes things happen on schedule." To do this, leaders must know exactly WHERE THEY

STAND and STAY IN CONTROL with constant FOLLOW-UP of every situation. They must know whether their people are succeeding or failing. They must correct errors immediately and must prevent similar mistakes from happening in the future. Effective control and follow-up should not be a police action.

The "do it or else" technique just won't get the results that POSITIVE CONTROL will. People do not resent a positive control system, in fact, they like it. They are stimulated and encouraged by it because they know exactly what is expected of them. As long as they do their work within certain guidelines, they do not have the FEAR of being reprimanded. People must be held accountable for their part of the overall results, otherwise people become lax and just coast along.

DELEGATION. The purpose of leading is not to do the job oneself, but to see to it that the job gets done effectively and on schedule. Thus, delegation is required. *When properly delegating, leaders extend themselves, thus creating growth.*

The first thing to keep in mind in delegating is not to delegate the task to be performed, but delegate the results to be achieved. Along with this you must also extend the *authority* to carry out the "delegation" and assign the *responsibility* for its accomplishment.

Don't delegate the CRUMBS . . . delegate the BREAD!

Successful delegation allows expansion and holds people accountable in a positive way. It also frees the leader's time so that the most important problems and matters can be concentrated on.

Ask yourself, "How much pressure am I under?" "Do I have time to do all the things I know ought to be done on my job?" "Am I so busy just keeping up that I don't have much time for thinking and planning about the future?"

Many leaders are too busy for their own good—and everyone

else's good. Everyone would be better off if they delegated a few chores to someone else and spent more time on the things which they alone can handle and will never get done unless they themselves do them.

When leaders are pressed for time they tend to concentrate on things which call for action *right now*. Consideration on long range goals and problems, which may be of equal or even greater importance, is postponed, sometimes indefinitely.

Being "too busy" sounds like a wonderful excuse. But it is a very poor reason for not getting around to matters which are vital to the future of the business. Leaders who are "too busy," who do not delegate intelligently, who do not keep themselves free to concentrate on the MOST IMPORTANT MATTERS, become a serious liability. Instead of delegating effectively and moving up the ladder of success, they are probably destined for a dead-end assignment . . . small enough to handle all by themselves.

CREATIVE AND IMAGINATIVE THINKING

In Hamilton, Ohio, some years ago, a struggling young manufacturer, named Herbert Piker, sat staring at a fisherman's minnow bucket (one bucket fits inside another). Suddenly he got an idea. Why not put insulation between those two cans? With ice cubes inside it would be a perfect picnic box to keep food and drinks cold.

That was the origin of the now-famous *Scotch Kooler*. In four years Piker's company jumped from a rundown maker of strong boxes—the business he had inherited from his father—to a concern grossing five million dollars a year.

Without imaginative and creative thinking, a person or a business can become stagnant. The bility to be creative and imaginative is one of the most sought-after qualities in a leader today. Creative thinking is largely a matter of attitude. You have to be open-minded . . . have an inquiring mind, never be satisfied, feeling that everything can be improved!

Have these questions constantly in mind—

Is there a better, faster, easier or cheaper way?

Can it be changed, combined, or improved?

Why is this necessary?

Here are some suggestions for developing your creative abilities:

1. Sell yourself on yourself.
2. Have an open-minded attitude.
3. Have happy discontentment.
4. Find the right time of the day for you.
5. Work on one thing at a time.
6. Keep the ideas flowing. Some of the best ideas come after you think you have exhausted all possibilities.
7. Don't care what others will say or think.
8. Don't stop in the middle of your creative session . . . evaluate the ideas later.
9. Pick a place where you can concentrate.
10. Set a goal—a definite target will help to stimulate ideas.
11. Give yourself a deadline.
12. Use your experience and best judgment to determine the best idea.

Ideas don't just happen. Like any other skill, creative thinking can be developed to a high degree of proficiency. The key to creative thinking is YOU and YOUR ATTITUDE.

Businesses, communities, and industries today are hungry for ideas and will reward the people who can supply them. Idea people are rare.

Keeping People Motivated and Morale High. In addition to

the ideas that have been discussed in this book up to this point, here are some other ideas to keep people highly motivated; thereby, helping the leader to obtain even more profitable action, to impel the other person to *want to* rather than feel he *has to:*

1. Become geniunely interested in every person.
2. Recognize and praise their achievements.
3. Make them feel that they and their work are important. Help them to see the total picture of which they are a part.
4. Respect their individuality. They are people, not just cogs in a machine or a number.
5. Stand behind them when they are right and offer constructive ideas when they are wrong.
6. Make sure they know what's expected of them . . . provide them with a "goal-oriented" job description.
7. Set an enthusiastic, optimistic example.
8. Get rid of the dead timber, the "aginers." Productive people do not like working around negatives.
9. Create a climate whereby people want to offer ideas and suggestions and recognize them when they do, showing them that you appreciate their contributions.
10. Keep the lines of communication open and let everyone know exactly how they stand.
11. Play no favorites.
12. Display an open-minded and listening attitude.
13. Practice empathy in all relationships.
14. Practice good human relations.
15. Create and maintain a climate of mutual trust, respect and confidence.
16. Compensate them adequately when they have produced expected results.

COMMUNICATION. Real leaders recognize that communication is not a separate activity but an essential part of everything that is being done. In addition to the vital points made on communication in Chapter 12, here are some additional suggestions for leaders:

It is a must to clearly communicate the goals to be achieved and the methods to be used in achieving them. Your people must understand the rules and limitations to be observed in achieving their goals so that they understand clearly what they may and may not do. EMPATHY must always be maintained in all communications and the FEED BACK must be observed and analyzed. Most job-related problems can be solved through adequate understanding, provided the understanding is based on two-way communication. It should be recognized that the most powerful communication is not always *what we say* BUT *what we do and what we are.*

DECISION MAKING AND PROBLEM SOLVING. I covered this in Chapter 13. However, I might add that leaders can rise no higher than the way that they can solve problems. They will be judged in the future not by their intentions, but by the decisions they have made and the problems they have solved.

ALWAYS LOOK FOR THE SIMPLEST SOLUTION THAT WILL BRING ADEQUATE RESULTS. Leaders consider decision making an opportunity to contribute to the overall goals. Their decisions help to advance their own career, the careers of others and the future of the business. They face difficult decisions head-on. *They try to find an opportunity in every crisis.* The leader is always motivated and motivates people to carry out and put decisions into action without procrastination.

YOU MUST EARN LOYALTY. Clarence Francis, while chariman of General Foods, best expressed this philosophy with these words: "You can buy a man's time, you can buy a man's physical presence at a given place, you can even buy a measured number of skilled, muscular motions per hour or per day. But you cannot buy enthusiasm, you cannot buy initiative, you cannot buy loyalty, you cannot buy the devotion of hearts, minds and souls. You have to earn these things . . .''

You cannot sell people on the idea of being loyal to you. You win their loyalty through exchange. You must demonstrate loyalty to people. You must win and earn their loyalty in response to your treatment of your people. Therefore, always lead from high principles, from that which is right, just and fair. This will engender a mutuality of interest that will generate and maintain loyalty.

TOWER OF STRENGTH. What do people look for in a true leader? A TRUE LEADER is a *tower of strength* because he or she inspires trust and confidence by his or her actions and words. He or she is self-disciplined and sets an excellent example at all times. He or she *builds* and *develops* people and motivates them to peak achievement. He or she has strong convictions that give a strong positive outlook and, even in the face of difficulties, has the ''It will be done'' attitude, imparting it to all of those around. He or she has drive and ambition and leads from a strong and determined purpose. *He or she welds people together into a profitable, well-coordinated, hard-hitting, result-getting team.*

▲   ▲   ▲   ▲

"GARDLINES" *by Grant G. Gard*

DON'T TALK ABOUT THESE THINGS—DO THEM NOW!!

1. Plot a FRESH and CREATIVE APPROACH to your leadership.
2. ADOPT THE ATTITUDE that with your leadership your people will produce desired results with your guidance, coaching and supervision.

3. Have a DEFINITE PLAN, including the three types of goals and the actions necessary to achieve them.
4. Get the RIGHT PEOPLE on the RIGHT JOB to produce maximum results, using peoples' highest skills and abilities.
5. Issue directives that AID IN GOAL ACHIEVEMENT and are not barriers to goal achievement.
6. Hold people accountable by POSITIVE CONTROL METHODS.
7. Expand your capabilities through EFFECTIVE DELEGATION.
8. Develop your CREATIVE ABILITIES.
9. MOTIVATE PEOPLE properly and KEEP MORALE HIGH for greatest productivity.
10. Lead by example—be a TOWER OF STRENGTH.
11. Constantly be BUILDING and DEVELOPING people.
12. Use POSITIVE COMMUNICATION in words, deeds and actions.
13. Look at decision making and problem solving as OPPORTU-NITIES to create growth.

▲   ▲   ▲   ▲

THOUGHT PROVOKING QUOTES

"Nothing is easier than fault-finding; no talent, no self-denial, no brains, no character are required to set up the grumbling business."
—Robert West

"Management by objectives works if you know the objectives. Ninety percent of the time you don't."
—Peter Drucker

"The unfortunate thing about the world is that good habits are so much easier to give up than bad ones."
—Somerset Maugham

"Genius is the ability to reduce the complicated to the simple."
—C. W. Ceram

"There can be no security where there is fear."
—Felix Frankfurter

"If you can believe, all things are possible to him who believes."
—Mark, 9:23

"One of the tests of leadership is the ability to recognize a problem before it becomes an emergency."
—Arnold H. Glasow

"It isn't the incompetent who destroy an organization. The incompetent never get in a position to destroy it. It is those who have achieved something and want to rest upon their achievements who are forever clogging things up."
—F. M. Young

"The most important thing in life is not to capitalize on your gains. Any fool can do that. The really important thing is to profit from your losses. That requires intelligence; and it makes the difference between a man of sense and a fool."
—William Bolitho

"I never knew an early rising, hard working, prudent man, careful of his earnings and strictly honest, who complained of bad luck. A good character, good habits and iron industry are impregnable to the assaults of all luck that fools ever dreamed of."
—Joseph Addison

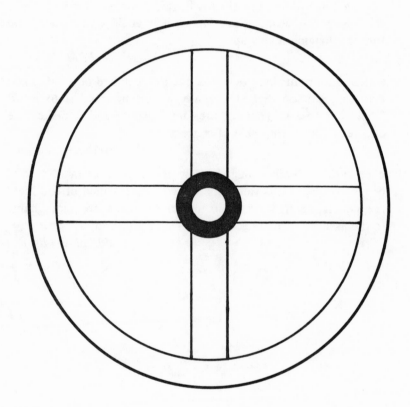

18 | *Wheel of Life*

The Four Ingredients. There are four powerful ingredients in the life of a successful person—success being defined as the realization of a worthy goal—one who obtains desired results with his or her life.

FIRST SPOKE—GOD

You and I need a Supreme Being to share our good times and bad times. I feel that *no life is complete without God.* When we get God and our religious outlook out of focus, everything is out of balance. God and a religious outlook on life give us the track and path to take for our inner happiness and achievement. We live in a world of faith and hope. Many times I think we "Ask God" for so much that we fail to "Thank God" for all of the many good things we have and the guidance He provides.

We can all thank God for the many opportunities we have every day of our lives; for the opportunity of making a living in the great country that has the Free Enterprise System where we do not have limitations placed on us; for our families, associates, churches, schools. I could go on and on.

I have been as "high" as any person on the face of this earth and I have been as "low." One of the greatest tragedies in my life happened September 24, 1971. My oldest son, Greg, age 17, an honor student at Billy Mitchell High School, was killed instantly in an automobile accident. I loved that boy! It was a great loss, a shock, a blow. I turned to God and I know that's where I got the strength to fight on. I knew that God loved me and I learned to put my faith and hope in God. I did everything possible to help myself.

I know that God will help us in our "LOW VALLEYS" and see us to "GREAT HEIGHTS" if we will just give Him an opportunity.

Carl Jung, one of the world's greatest psychiatrists of all time wrote, "During the past 30 years, people from all the civilized countries over Europe have consulted me. I have treated many hundreds of patients. Among all my patients over the age of 35, there was not one whose problems, in the final analysis, was not that of finding a religious outlook on life. It is safe to say, then, that every one of them fell ill because they lost that which the living religions of every age had given to their followers . . . and I would say that not one patient in 30 years under my care was ever really healed unless he regained a healthy, religious outlook."

A scientist thought prayer was humbug. He became ill, came close to bankruptcy and many of his experiments failed. One day, mostly to get away from home, he want to the shrine. "If I were not an agnostic, I might experiment with this superstition." Convincing himself he was going through the motions out of curiosity, he started the ritual. Half way through, he thought, "Now, if this were not folly, what would I pray for? Health? Money? He suddenly cried, 'Oh, God, I beg you, enlighten my mind so I may invent something very great to further human knowledge!' "

Amazed, the scientist stood in silence. So this was his desire of desires. Knowing it at last, Galileo began experiments which led to the invention of the telescope.

SECOND SPOKE—SELF

Everything in life starts with SELF. Have a GOOD SELF-IMAGE, a real good SELF-WORTH. Be glad you are you. Like yourself and see yourself becoming the type of person you really want to become. *You always get back exactly what you send out!!* Erase self-doubt and control fear. Act confidently and enthusiastically. Look at things optimistically . . . that every door has hinges and handles, not latches and locks.

Analyze your past objectively and PROFIT FROM EVERY EXPERIENCE. A suburbanite put on a last minute spurt of speed to catch his train—but he missed it. A bystander remarked, "If you had just run a little faster you would have made it." The suburbanite replied, "No, it wasn't a case of running faster, but of starting sooner."

Yes, look at yourself objectively and let past experiences be a foundation for your growth in the future.

I love the advice of Elbert Hubbard which I am quoting. If every person would apply it and live by the wisdom contained in it, he or she would be an even happier, more successful person.

"Whenever you go out of doors, draw the chin in, carry the crown of the head high and fill the lungs to the utmost; drink in the sunshine; greet your friends with a smile and put soul into every handclasp. Do not fear being misunderstood and do not waste a minute thinking about your enemies. Try to fix firmly in your mind what you would like to do, and then, without veering of direction, you will move straight to the goal. Keep your mind on the great and splendid things you would like to do, and then, as the days go gliding by, you will find yourself unconsciously seizing upon the opportunities that are required for the fulfillment of your desire, just as the coral insect takes from the running tide the elements it needs. Picture in your mind the able, earnest, useful person you desire to be, and the thought you hold is hourly transforming you into that particular individual . . . Thought is supreme. Preserve a right mental attitude—the attitude of courage, frankness and good cheer. To think rightly is to create. All things come through desire and every sincere prayer is answered. We become like that on which our hearts are fixed. Carry your chin in and the crown of your head high. We are gods in the chrysalis.''

EXPECT THE BEST AND GET IT

Aim high when setting worthy, realistic goals and have great expectations. Sure, everyone should expect to meet some difficulties, some problems and challenges along the way, but with a positive attitude about ourselves, and knowing that difficulties are opportunities for us to succeed, we can achieve our great expectations.

THIRD SPOKE—OTHERS

The one common denominator to all success and happiness is other people. You can get the things you want in life if you help enough other people get what they want. Regardless of our profession, WE ARE IN THE PEOPLE BUSINESS. There are several essential qualities in dealing with people successfully: Sincerity; integrity; empathy; and enthusiasm. These are the qualities that enable us to obtain DESIRED RESULTS working with and through people.

THINK OTHER PEOPLE ARE IMPORTANT

The very first basic rule is have the sincere attitude that other people are important. This puts your human relations on a very sincere and heartfelt basis. The deepest craving every person has is the craving *to be appreciated* and *to feel important.* You can't make the other person feel important if you secretly feel that person is a "nobody."

Dr. Rhine of Duke University said, "Our treatment of people obviously depends on *what we think they are,* as does our treatment of everything else. No other way would be intelligent. Our feelings for people depend on our ideas about them."

Men and women who are the happiest and who have the most influence with other people are men and women who CARE ABOUT OTHERS and who BELIEVE OTHER PEOPLE ARE IMPORTANT and every one of their attitudes, actions and feelings radiate these qualities honestly and sincerely.

To work successfully with anyone, whether it be a child, a customer, an associate, an employee or a friend, here are 5 check points of great importance: Did I leave that OTHER PERSON *respecting me, trusting me, liking me, believing me, admiring me?* Happiness and achievement always come to the man or woman who accomplishes this with OTHERS.

YOU ENRICH YOUR OWN LIFE WHEN YOU ENRICH THE LIVES OF OTHERS.

FOURTH SPOKE—LOVE

Elbert Hubbard said, "Get your happiness out of your work, or you may never know what happiness is." In order to really succeed and be happy we must LOVE PEOPLE and LOVE OUR WORK. If we don't love both, we are in trouble.

An insurance company was having a hard time making one of its branch offices pay. It was in the "red" and had gone through six managers who were not able to turn it around. Finally, management decided to try a young man who had a good record. At the end of one year, he had a dozen salespeople working for him and had written more insurance than had been written in the last five years combined. The office was in the "black" . . . the first time it had really been profitable. The top management called this young fellow into the home office and asked him the secret of his success. It was, "First, you must love what you are doing. Second, you have to love people, but, more important, they have to know that you feel that way about them!"

We can't hide our attitude about how we feel about anything or anybody. We must "give out love" before we can expect to "get it back." When we really *love people* and *love the thing we are doing,* that's when we operate the best—and that's when we are the happiest.

I heard the story of the church meeting when one parishioner gave a large sum of money as a donation to the church. Another parishioner said, "He's got it, so he gave it." The minister said, "I don't know about that statement, 'he's got it, so he gave it,' I believe that *he gave it* and that's the reason *he's got it!*"

So true . . . when we *love,* we *give* of ourselves. When we *give* of ourselves, we have a *better attitude.* When we have a *better attitude,* we are *more productive* and *enjoy life more.* LOVE and GIVE!! The rewards will follow in many ways.

BE PROUD TO BE A "WILLER"

Three kinds of people. Having spoken to and trained thousands of men and women from all walks of life, I know that there are three distinct types of people in this world:

1. The Wills. 2. The Won'ts. 3. The Can'ts.

The "Wills" accomplish everything! They are the "DOERS." The "Won'ts" oppose everything, they fight progress and new ideas. The "Can'ts" fail at everything.

Be a "WILL" type person and achieve the things you want in your life. It's all up to you! Any person can see further than he or she can reach, so that means that you should keep reaching. Always be reaching for some worthwhile goal. The greatest achievements of mankind have been accomplished by two types of people: Those who were smart enough to know it could be done; and those too dumb to know it couldn't!!

FIGHT ONE MORE ROUND

James J. Corbett said, "When your feet are so tired that you have to shuffle back to the center of the ring, *fight one more round.* When your arms are so tired that you can hardly lift your hands to come on guard, *fight one more round.* When your nose is bleeding and your eyes are black and you are so tired that you wish your opponent would crack you one on the jaw and put you to sleep, *fight one more round*—remembering that the man who always fights one more round is never whipped."

YOU HAVE EVERYTHING YOU REALLY WANT

I am going to close this book exactly the way I opened it. Right now, everyone one of us has everything we really want in the way of happiness and achievement. I didn't say "dreamed about" and I didn't say "wished for . . . I said "REALLY WANT." I believe every man and woman on the face of this earth has the potential to do exactly with their lives the thing that they really want to do. People are as happy as they set their minds to be. People accomplish exactly what they set their minds to achieve.

I hope that in between the opening statement and the closing statement of this book, I have given you some practical ideas to help you live a richer, happier and an even more successful life. This is my goal and my prayer in writing this book.

I firmly believe that with the INGREDIENTS of the WHEEL OF LIFE your goals can and will become a reality. *You must be right with God, you must be right with yourself, you must be right with others,* and *love life to the fullest.* Every principle discussed in this book somehow relates to these four qualities, the qualities that help the *very determined person to find a way to great accomplishments in life!*

▲ ▲ ▲ ▲

"GARDLINES" *by Grant G. Gard*

DON'T TALK ABOUT THESE THINGS—DO THEM NOW!!

1. Form a PARTNERSHIP with God.
2. Have a GOOD SELF-IMAGE. Like yourself.
3. ANALYZE and PROFIT from your past experiences.
4. EXPECT THE BEST and get it.
5. ALWAYS use empathy, integrity, sincerity and enthusiasm in working with people.
6. Realize you must "GIVE IT" before you are going to "GET IT."
7. LOVE your profession, job, family, people and life to the fullest.
8. Be proud to be a "WILLER."

▲ ▲ ▲ ▲

THOUGHT PROVOKING QUOTES

"People do not lack strength, they lack will."
                                        —*Victor Hugo*

"There is no genius in life like the genius of energy and industry."

—Mitchell

"Trust men and they will be true to you; treat them greatly and they will show themselves great."

—Emerson

Twelve Things to Remember
1. The value of time.
2. The success of perseverance.
3. The pleasure of working.
4. The dignity of simplicity.
5. The worth of character.
6. The power of kindness.
7. The influence of example.
8. The obligation of duty.
9. The wisdom of economy.
10. The virtue of patience.
11. The improvement of talent.
12. The joy of originating.

—Marshall Field

"At all costs we must re-establish faith in spiritual values. We must worship something beyond ourselves, lest we destroy ourselves."

—Philip Gibbs

"I know there is a Supreme Being who rules the affairs of men and whose goodness and mercy have always followed the American people and I know He will not turn from us now if we humbly and reverently seek His powerful aid."

—Grover Cleveland

"Without Divine assistance I can not succeed; with it I can not fail."

—Abraham Lincoln

"It's good to have money and the things that money can buy, but it's good, too, to check up once in a while and make sure you haven't lost the things that money can't buy."

—George Horace Lorimer

"Happiness is a perfume you cannot pour on others without getting a few drops on yourself."

—Ralph Waldo Emerson

"Dear God, give us strength to accept with serenity the things that cannot be changed. Give us the courage to change the things that can and should be changed. And give us the wisdom to distinguish one from the other."

—Admiral Thomas C. Hart

"I thank God for my handicaps for, through them, I have found myself, my work and my God."

—Helen Keller

"Be willing to have it so. Acceptance of what has happened is the first step to overcoming the consequences of any misfortune."

—William James

"The ideal man bears the accidents of life with dignity and grace, making the best of the circumstances."

—Aristotle

"I believe God is managing affairs and that He doesn't need any advice from me. With God in charge, I believe everything will work out for the best in the end. So what is there to worry about?"

—Henry Ford

"The four cornerstones of character on which the structure of this nation was built are: Initiative, Imagination, Individuality and Independence."

—Capt. Edward Rickenbacker

"For one man who sincerely pities our misfortunes, there are a thousand who sincerely hate our success."

—Charles C. Colton